Song Of Hope

Song Of Hope

Kathy Moore

The publisher and the author recognize and accept that the final authority regarding these experiences rests with the Holy See of Rome, to whose judgement we willingly submit.

- The publisher and the author

Printed in the United States of America

Cover design by Maria Trimbell

Coyote Publishing
P.O. Box 1854
Yreka, California   96097
Voice-Mail/FAX: 530 842-5788

coyote@snowcrest.net

Library of Congress Catalog Card Number: 99-72141

ISBN: 0-9628801-9-1

Published by:
Coyote Publishing
A self-publishing company that reflects the author's unique style.

Acknowledgements

This book would not be possible without the help of the Holy Trinity; Father, Son, and Holy Spirit and all those in Heaven and on Earth who have been praying for me, that God reveal Himself to me, to touch my heart and change it, to give me boldness in proclaiming my experiences.

I wish to thank everyone who helped me in any way, shape or form, by proof reading this book, by offering words of encouragement, by praying that it be published, and I ask God's blessings upon each one of them.

I thank my pastor and my spiritual director, who permitted the Holy Spirit to guide them and thus me.

I thank Charlie Knecht, Director of Friday Night with Jesus Ministries, who accepted my writing for his newsletter, and suggested that my experiences be placed in a book.

I thank my sister, Carol. When I was very sick and said, "If the doctor says I have six months to live, I am going to quit my job and write," she responded, "If I were you and the doctor said that I have forty years to live, I would quit my job and write." She also helped proof read my book.

To Bill Walker, a friend of my dad's, who read my account of the Flanagan family history, Roses in December, and wrote me a letter to follow my dream and talent and write.

I thank my friend, Linda Perkins, who also proof read my book, and the members of the Trinity Prayer Community for their prayers and support.

I thank Father Armand Nigro, SJ, who consented to read my book, and then voluntarily wrote the Foreword and offered editorial comments.

I thank my friend, Shari Fiock, Publisher of Coyote Publishing, who has encouraged my writing for many years.

I wish to especially thank two friends who encouraged me and prayed for me but who passed away before this book reached press, author William Diehm, a great motivator, and my best friend, Marilyn Calliari.

Dedication

To the Most Holy Trinity God
The Father, Son, and Holy Spirit
The Source of All
Life, Love, and Wisdom

Contents

Foreword

God communicates with us in countless ways — through creation, through His Church and its loving ministries of the Word, the Sacraments, and services to the needy; through events of our sacred history and individual lives, and through Holy Scripture. God also speaks to us through uniquely chosen individuals, to whom He reveals Himself and through whom He continues to speak to us. We call them God's prophets.

Prophets are not only featured in Hebrew and Christian Bibles, but are men and women down the ages who hear God's message and try to discern and communicate it as faithfully as possible to the rest of us. They are convinced that God calls them to do this.

The experience of God's presence and activity, of God's absolute goodness and unconditional love — any such human experience which I call God-experience — initiated and sustained by God, is mystical experience. All genuine mysticism is God-initiated human experience. We humans cannot produce or sustain or merit any of it. It is totally God's gift. People habitually or often gifted with such experiences are "mystics". Human initiated and sustained religious activity is called asceticism, and the human agents of such activity are "ascetics."

Mystics are almost always normal, ordinary people who have done nothing to deserve such graces. Usually, though, they are more aware of their spiritual poverty and weaknesses and need of God than are others.

Throughout human history God has enriched his people through these prophets and mystics. We say they are "charismatic" (God-gifted).

I have carefully read this manuscript of Kathy Moore and have made only minor stylistic suggestions and offered rarely a theological term or clarification, careful not to change what she intended to write.

I have read her testimony of God, her very cautious attempt to articulate what God has done for her and for others through her. I have spent some 40 years teaching Sacred Scripture and Christian Spirituality, directing retreats and serving as a Spiritual director. I find Kathy's writings, though uniquely hers, very consistent with the prophetic and mystical traditions of our Judeo-Christian faith, and with the teachings of our Church.

Except for one phone conversation, I have never met Kathy Moore; but if she had been coming to me for spiritual direction with these writings and interpretations of her God-experiences, I would have said to her, "Kathy, this sounds like the God I know. Continue to let God be and do and say to you whatever He wants. Continue to ask God to enlighten and reveal to you His preferences for your choices and conduct, and to empower you to carry out His preferences — including your writings."

Read on and meet Kathy's God, the Father, Son and Holy Spirit, who through the life, death and resurrection of Jesus of Nazareth, the Son of Mary, lives on in us, sharing their divine life with us, fashioning us into his beloved family. May this manuscript have many unending readers in days and years to come, and may they meet anew the one and only God of surprises, the God of absolute goodness, constantly active in our lives, who loves each and all of us uniquely with unconditional love.

Fr. Armand M. Nigro S.J., Professor of Religious Studies
Gonzaga University, Spokane, WA
Queenship of Mary, our Mother
August 22, 1997

Introduction

I write this book of happenings to give my testimony, to be a witness, to encourage people to speak about their experiences, to help others grow in their faith, to affirm those who are seeking confirmation of their beliefs.

I am not alone in experiencing the Manifestations of God's Presence in our lives. The more bold I tell others of my experiences, the more people open their hearts to me with their stories. God is touching uncounted people every day.

God removed my fears. I hope this book will help remove fears so others will turn to God in hope.

God has showered me with Gifts, the greatest and most awesome is the Gift of Himself, of His love for me; and then the gift of my grateful, loving response. It is beyond anything I have ever felt before, anything I have ever imagined.

I cannot prove any of the experiences I have written. It is my word against all who roll their eyes. Those who have had similar experiences will know I speak the truth. Those who know me know I speak the truth.

I know the attitudes and feelings I have had in the past compared to those I have now. My feelings of bitterness and hate have turned to forgiveness and love. It is beyond me, beyond my humanness, beyond my understanding. How I loved God before was like a drop of water compared to the ocean of love God has given me. I know this love overflows to all around me. I know that I have changed much, that my faith, my hope, my love in and for God has grown. I know I merit none of this. Why has this happened to me and not to others? Only God knows. Maybe they have not desired it. Maybe they don't believe it to be possible. Maybe I needed it more than they. But it happened to me, and it can happen to you.

I have included a few simple prayers. God manifested His Presence to me so that I would turn to Him and grow in my faith. I do not say, "Do this, pray that!" God takes each of us on our own journey. I do know this. God is love. In the goodness of the Lord all shall know Him. Turn to Him in prayer. Believe in Him. He will help you trust in Him.

To the Reader:

I heard the voice of God. It was a man's voice. In this manner He manifested His presence to me.

I also experienced God through the cloud of forgetting, into the cloud of unknowing. I realize just saying or writing G-O-D is limiting God. To say He is the Creator, just by saying it, limits Him, for He is beyond all He created. To say He is Truth, just by saying it, limits Him, for He is beyond all Truth known to mankind. To say He is Love, is limiting Him, for He is beyond all Love known to us. We have not seen nor heard nor can we even imagine all that God is. To me, God is the Great Unknown, beyond all our knowledge.

I cannot adequately define God at all. To go into all this detail each time I refer to Him would make my book extremely long and tedious. Instead, I will attempt to describe my experiences with God, beyond all mere human experience and thus beyond words. I will also limit God by describing Him with masculine words, for that is how He manifested His presence to me.

TRUST IN THE LORD

We have all felt being loved by someone — the love of our parents, our spouse, our children, our grandchildren. The first time I felt the love of God was when Father John Campoli prayed over me.

The stress in my life had become so great I could barely think. I could not sleep nights. It had been maybe five years since I had a good night's sleep. My brain took forever to process information. I could almost feel it go from brain cell to brain cell to find the right information. It seemed there was a shield coming down over the front of my brain.

In order to walk, I had to think left, right, left, right. As I went slower, of course my boss wanted me to go faster. She would ask me a question and be able to walk across the room before I could process the answer. She was very fast thinking; so my slowness would irritate her. My slow answers embarrassed me, thus slowing down the thinking process even more.

I was an accountant for a non-profit organization. I devised my own computer program to keep track of the various fund accounts. Their income and expenses totaled over $500,000 per year and my records were accurate to the penny. I was able to produce a print-out of all expenses within minutes, but my boss deemed the program too slow. She brought in several CPA people who went over everything I did. In the meantime, I had to jot down my activity every fifteen minutes. The team of accountants said I should be able to do all the records, keep track of the budget of all the directors, do payroll, etc, in twenty hours a week. My time card showed that was exactly how much time I spent on the books.

I only worked part-time and was not allowed overtime, just comp. time. If I had to attend a board meeting in the evening, I had three hours less during the week to get my normal work done. I just could not keep up. The faster I tried to go, the more I shut down and the slower I went.

Pain was a constant in my life. Every muscle hurt. I had already spent several years going to a chiropractor and could no longer afford the expense. I learned to live with the pain.

The threat of losing my job hung over my head daily and I thought the end of the world would come if I lost it.

Many emotional hurts in my life were now taking their toll. I read somewhere that it takes about one year to recover from every five years of stress. I had been married fifteen years. I was now a single parent and I had never given myself time to heal after the divorce. Now I was experiencing stress on my job as well.

My pain grew. I began to have pains in my chest and abdomen. After spending thousands of dollars on hospital tests which found nothing and provided no hope of relief from the medical profession, I turned in desperation to God.

"Please help me", I begged on my knees at two in

the morning as tears ran down my face. That's all I could say. I couldn't pray in a specific way on how I wanted help. But God knew what I needed.

Shortly after this, on a Tuesday, May 5 to be exact, I listened to a self-improvement tape and the speaker asked, "What do you want to do most in your life? Deep down, what answer comes to mind?"

My answer was, "I want to write."

The voice continued, "That is also what God wants you to do."

This was new to me. I had always thought what you wanted God didn't want! A deep sense of peace came over me, and I knew I had to follow my dream and write. But this was a major decision to make. All creativity stopped when I got a divorce. I stopped reading novels, I stopped creating sculptures, I stopped sewing, needle-work, I stopped writing letters. I compensated by switching to the left side of my brain and studied accounting. Writing is not something I did, it was something I longed to do. Writing was not an acceptable profession to my family and friends. The desire to write was something I had kept hidden within me all my life. To realize this desire, to realize it was deep within me, that writing was me, to make the decision to follow this dream, was a very major move to make.

That same day (Tuesday, May 5) someone phoned and said a world-renowned healing priest was coming to our small parish on Friday night. I thought, "I would rather do anything than go to Mass on a day I don't have to. I'd rather watch marshmallows puff up in the microwave than go to Mass!" But suddenly I had the impression God was talking to me through this person.

3

Song of Hope

All day Friday the thought kept running through my mind, "Tonight my life is going to change forever." The thought wasn't *"Today"* my life is going to change forever, or even "this noon" but *"tonight"*. At noon I met with my boss and we parted company.

That night I went to Father John Campoli's healing Mass. As he prayed over me, I felt him push me. Nothing happened that I was aware of, but I was drawn to this man's spirituality and returned the following night. Again I felt this "push". As I left the church I thought, "that's the end of that". I had prayed that my mind would be healed so I could think again and I offered my hands to Him for my writing and my lips for my speaking.

I want to interject and point out some words I said in the above paragraph. "Nothing happened that I was aware of". God was already beginning to work within me. I offered my mind, hands and lips for my use. At a later date, Father Campoli prayed over me and I felt him "push" me. I resisted this push so much I was leaning backwards at a 45 degree angle. I then opened my eyes and saw Father Campoli's hands were not anywhere near me. I then realized I had to let go and trust. This "push" was feeling the Presence of the Holy Spirit.

The following Saturday (May 16) my friend called several of us to the church and asked us to recite the consecration prayer to the Sacred Heart of Jesus and the Immaculate Heart of Mary. As a Catholic, I had read this prayer numerous times throughout my life without giving it much thought. But when I looked at it this time, I thought, "This is serious! This is a commitment.

Do I want to do this?" I immediately said, "Yes," and said the prayer. Then I learned Father Campoli was still in the area. He was saying Mass at 2 p.m. in a church two hours away. Two hours! I didn't want to drive two hours when church was just five minutes from my home! But this person needed a ride. She had prayed for this healing priest to come to our area and now that he was here, her car was giving her trouble. Through clenched teeth I said, "All right. I'll drive you to Grant's Pass."

The next day this person was too sick to go to the healing Mass. (It is amazing how many people are too sick to go to a healing Mass!) I found myself getting ready to go by myself. I asked "Why?" And this voice inside me said, "Trust in me." I asked, "Will I fall?" for people fell when Father prayed over them. This voice said, "Trust in me." I said, "You know I can believe in You, I can hope in You, I can love You, but You know I cannot trust You." The voice inside me said, "Trust in ME." I went to Grant's Pass.

I did not know where the Catholic church was. Nearing the exit of Grant's Pass I passed a little red sports car with numerous religious stickers in the window. I wondered if they were going to this Charismatic healing Mass. I do not even know why I thought these people were Catholic. My only experience so far had been with very conservative Catholics and they would not have religious stickers in their windows. The Catholics I knew didn't broadcast the fact that they knew Jesus. I had not yet met a Charismatic Catholic.

I kept watching this little red sports car in my rear view mirror and I passed the first exit to Grant's Pass. Having no idea how many exits there were I

almost passed the second (and last) exit when they
turned on their car's signal lights. I quickly exited,
watching them in my mirror. They turned off to the left.
I went one more block, turned left and circled back to
find them again. They drove right to the Catholic church.

At the end of the Mass, I went to have Father
pray over me. When it was my turn, he pulled me close
and hugged me. I couldn't have fallen if I wanted to! I
sat down in the pew and suddenly the whole church
disappeared and I was alone with God. I knew I was
being hugged by God. A wonderful feeling of peace and
happiness came over me.

When I became aware of my surroundings, the
service was over and the last song of praise was being
sung. Father was by the altar singing and dancing to
the praise music. I looked at his face which radiated
God's love, and I watched his body move to God's love.
I thought of my own face which showed no emotion
whatsoever for fear of being hurt again. I looked down
at my body, held rigid because of the many walls I had
built around me. My hands were in tight fists down by
my sides. I looked again at Father's radiant face and
prayed, "Lord, I want what he has. I want my face to
radiate Your love and I want my body to move and
dance to Your love."

Six weeks later I saw Father Campoli again on a
retreat in Sacramento. I related to him how Jesus had
come into me, filling me with wave after wave of love.
But I am getting ahead of myself. I will describe in
detail how, in six short weeks, God took away all my
pain. With one stroke He slashed away the barriers and
began healing my painful memories. The voice inside

me said, "I have taken away your pain. Now learn from me to heal yourself."

I could not experience God and not change. I began to spend two hours a day in prayer. I started saying the 45-day novena rosary and I attended Mass as daily as I could during the week for I began to believe receiving Jesus Christ under the appearance of bread and wine is the greatest prayer one can say. Remember, before this I considered myself lucky to get to Mass on Sundays.

In Father Campoli's speech he said to ask God for everything, to say, "I want it all." And so I did. As I learned to trust Him, He took away my fears of the future, of failing. Daily He showers me with love. And thus I learn to trust Him more.

I can now move easily, freely. My feelings and emotions are alive. As I lift my arms in praise to God, as my body sways to the music of praise and worship, I thank Him that I can once more feel and move and love again. Our God is an awesome God! As He makes His presence known to me in a very personal way, I wonder, "Why me?" I mean, God hugged me! God loves me! *And it is awesome.*

God loves each and every one of us. He calls us to love Him. "Love the Lord, thy God, with your whole heart and with your whole mind and with your whole soul."

Jesus Christ, Son of the living God, fill me with Your Holy Spirit and enable me to love.

Song of Hope

LAUGH

LAUGH, it's funny.
Yes. I'm laughing.
Somewhere deep inside,
Beneath all the pain
I'm laughing.

My hurt is buried deep within me
Closed in by a thick wall
A thick wall of non-emotion.
The pain only shows when you look deep into my eyes.
When I'm alone
A tear runs down my cheek.

Who would understand my pain?
Who would understand my hurt?

My wall is getting so high,
So thick around me,
It hurts to breathe.
My chest hurts.
I dare not move.
Someone will see and hurt me more.

My smile is gone.
No emotion plays across my features.
My feelings are hidden -
I think. But mirrors and cameras
Show me what others see.
They see my eyes and the pain.
The eyes betray.

CALLED TO MEDJUGORJE

Several years before I was Baptized in the Spirit I was called to Medjugorje. When the Virgin Mary ends her messages with, "Thank you for having responded to my call," that is exactly what she means. I first read about Medjugorje in a <u>Reader's Digest</u> magazine about 1985. In that town, in what was then Yugoslavia, several young visionaries were claiming to see the Blessed Virgin Mary at the same time every day and had been since June, 1981. I believed the story as soon as I read it.

At that time I thought, "Kathy, go to Medjugorje." Oh, no. People are seeing Mary and having miracles happen to them. This won't happen to me and I can't take that kind of rejection right now.

A while later I again thought, "Kathy, go to Medjugorje." Oh, no. I can pray to Mary just as well here in California as I can in Yugoslavia.

Then the divorce came. The divorce books recommend the first Christmas be spent doing something different so the children don't dwell on the traditional. I had the boys with me the first Christmas and we flew to Texas to be with my parents. The next Christmas I was to be alone, and so I decided to follow the advice of the book and do something completely different by myself. My roots are from Ireland and I decided to go there and walk the land my ancestors walked.

Song of Hope

That summer of 1989 as I was going out the door, there was my cat, Thomas, lying on the top step. As I was about to step over him a voice inside me said, "Kathy, pick up that cat, and hold it, and love it, for you will never see it again." Oh, I was too busy. I got in my car and drove away, and I never saw Thomas again. Shortly after that, very loud, very clear, this voice inside me said, "Kathy, go to Medjugorje. And bring your camera." I was not going to argue. Medjugorje became part of my travel plans. But I didn't tell people why. How could I say, "I heard this voice inside me tell me to go." Oh sure.

I don't think such thoughts. I don't worry about my sons before they take off in the car. I don't have premonitions that something might happen. This thought came so suddenly into my mind, "Pick up that cat and hold it and love it...", it was, to me, definitely a voice speaking within me.

I arrived in Medjugorje as a typical tourist with my camera around my neck, out of its case, ready to take a picture of the miraculous. It was cold and rainy. No place to go but to church. I never sat so long in a church before! I spent five hours at a time in there!

I saw many people crying. Why were they crying in this Holy place, I wondered?

There was a small chapel off from the main altar. People began to come out of this room, the door was open, so I went in. The pressure inside that room was unbearable! It was like sitting in a Volkswagen and slamming the doors - only twenty times greater. I couldn't stand it! I turned around and left. Since then I have come to call this pressure I felt, "the Power of God's Presence". I realize now I was not worthy to be within this feeling

Presence and yet, God gave me the gift to feel His Power, His Presence, in order to draw me to Himself.

As I sat in the church I soon found myself crying for no reason. One of the first signs of God's presence in your life is the Gift of Tears, tears of healing, tears of repentance.

When I went to Medjugorje, I had no intention to go to confession, but suddenly I had the desire. It was the first time in fifteen years. The lines were very long. I found a very short one, only two people were in front of me. After half an hour, only one had gone in. I had things to do, things to see, so I left. Later I joined another line. The same thing. I ended up going to confession to a priest I met there and learned why confessions were so long. The priests knew they had half an hour to talk the people into coming back to the Sacraments. I listened and didn't argue, but felt the priest just didn't understand the problems of getting to church when you were a single parent. I worked all week and the weekends were spent cleaning house, being with my boys and fixing up my property. Even though I was interiorly arguing, God was planting the seed of the importance of attending Mass.

Medjugorje is noted for the miracles of inner healing. It is a place where people of all nations, all religions, join together to pray in one building. It is a place where, if you go and stay longer than five days, your life will change forever. I was there five days.

I heard many stories of people going, wondering if their loved ones were in Heaven. The visionaries would single these people out and give them a personal message from Mary. I heard of people being physically healed. I also heard of rosaries turning gold. I did not expect a

miracle to happen to me. They happened to other people.
So as not to be disappointed, I bought a wooden rosary.

I climbed Holy Cross Hill. The path is wide and
well marked, yet I lost it and traveled alone up the back
of the mountain. My prayer was that my mind would
clear, that I could think and talk faster. I heard the voice
inside me say, "Then you will have both feet in your
mouth and not just one."

I asked, "Why was 'bring your camera' part of the
message?" Was God going to show up in my pictures?
I had heard of miraculous photos taken at Medjugorje.
People returned home, developed their film and there
was Mary in the church above the heads of everyone. Or
Saints' faces peered out from the vines behind the
visionaries. The answer came, "You take pictures of
empty churches, empty statues. Take pictures of people.
People honoring My mother." I began taking pictures of
people.

I talked to other people and found myself telling
how I was called there. As I told my story, they stood
nodding their heads, for they, too, had been called the
same way. Their arguments were the same, "I can't
afford such a trip...I can pray to Mary at home just as
much as I can in some foreign country," as they fought
against the call.

In the evening of Christmas day I joined hundreds
of other pilgrims on Apparition Hill. It was dark, so I
have no idea how many people were there. A voice
announced everyone be quiet and please, no pictures or
flashlights, as the apparition was about to take place. As
everyone became quiet, my heart suddenly felt as if a
fist clutched it. It was not a frightening feeling, nor was

it painful. The translator's voice spoke out of the darkness saying Mary had appeared dressed in gold and carried the child Jesus. She said we were all called there for a reason, to bring the message of Medjugorje to our homes: the message to pray, to fast, to be converted. By converted she meant to turn our lives daily towards God. She would be with us and help us with the words as we talked to others.

The next evening in the church I again felt a fist clutching my heart. Suddenly I knew I was feeling the presence of Mary. This was a special and very unexpected gift I received.

To experience the manifestation of God's Presence is a Gift from God. To know this experience is from God is another Gift. To understand the experience is yet another Gift. These gifts may be given simultaneously or years apart. At Medjugorje God gave me the Gift of feeling the presence of Mary on Apparition Hill and in the church, and of feeling the Power of His Presence when I went into the side Chapel.

These experiences of God are personal. No one can take them from me nor do you have to believe them. God draws each of us to Him in a unique way, in our own way, according to our needs.

Eternal Father, please grant me the Gift
of the knowledge of Your Presence in my life.

SUBMISSION

"Submit" to the Lord. When you turn to God, you have to "submit" to Him. After I was Baptized in the Spirit I kept hearing and reading this phrase. Oh, how I hated those words! To me, "submit" was the worst word in the English language. A woman submitted to her rapist. A woman submitted to her husband and all dreams died. How could I possibly submit to God?

I went to bed thinking about this word. "Well, OK. If that is what God wants. OK." I flung my arms out wide and said, "OK, God. I submit myself to You." Then I began saying the rosary.

During the third decade a feeling of heat and of love began to flow within me. I could feel this flow all through me, out my arms, out to the ends of my fingers, up into my face, forcing my face muscles upwards into a smile, shooting out my eyes. I felt wave after wave of this love flowing through me. A voice entered my thoughts, "Kathy. I love you."

I just about melted!!! I can say those words now, write those words and they do nothing to me, but that night, that voice spoken within me saying, "Kathy, I love you," filled me with complete happiness.

The voice continued in my thoughts, "Thank you for saying the rosary and honoring my mother."

With those words I promised I'd say it every day of my life!

"Now put on your scapular."

Oh, no. I will move and this will all be a dream and everything will go away!

The rosary and the scapular go together, like a shoe and sock. I had been given a scapular at Medjugorje, had worn it for three days and, not liking things around my neck, took it off. When I started saying the 54-day novena rosary I was told to wear my scapular. I hunted and hunted for this scapular. It had been several years since I had gone to Medjugorje and I had forgotten where I put it. Finally I said a prayer and found it immediately. I again wore it for three days and then took it off. I placed it on my nightstand by my bed.

Now this voice inside me was telling me to put it on. I got up, put it on and then nestled back down under my covers.

The feeling was still there!

The voice continued, "Now let me teach you about the word, 'submissive.'" It is the attitude of being a Best Friend - His Best Friend. You do things alike and together. You do what the other wants because you want to please Him. It is like traveling with your best friend. You may not want to see some sight, but she does, so you go and see it, and vice-versa.

"It is like being on a team - which you are - and you must follow the coach's orders in order to win. It is like being in the army - which you are - in which you must be submissive to your commander to be part of a victorious unit.

"A submissive position while lying in bed is feet nearly together but comfortable, arms at your side. At first your hands will be turned upwards but as you completely relax, the hands will turn down and can be placed on your chest. Your prayer should be a quiet conversation - a talk between you and Him."

Before this experience happened I never knew that people could feel God's love or hear His voice in this manner. I had never before read the life of a saint nor their writings describing their encounters with God.

Shortly after this lesson on submission, I was drawn into deep, passive contemplative prayer. The first time I experienced this I was sitting at the computer, when suddenly I lost all energy. My mind went completely blank, except for the word, "pray". I went and laid down since I no longer had the energy to sit. The feeling of the Presence of the Holy Spirit came over me and I laid thus for several hours. My mind would be blank, except every once in a while a phrase such as, "Holy, holy Lord. You are God almighty," would come to my mind. I knew I was praying, but I had never heard of praying without words before. I did not know what I was experiencing. Someone mentioned the word, "contemplative" prayer and I was drawn to it. Was this what I was experiencing?

I read a book on the subject, "Open Hearts, Open Minds" by Thomas Keating, which was on the subject of contemplative prayer, but it didn't describe how one felt when one experienced contemplative prayer. I just wasn't sure.

When earthquakes were occurring in Southern California, my friend's children were there and together we realized that every time they were being thrown about in the house, I was in this prayer state. One time the daughter was sitting inside the house against the patio glass doors when the earthquake started. She found herself outside, safe and sound and without a scratch, yet the glass in the door was shattered.

I experienced two different types of feeling. One I call the Presence of the Holy Spirit, which is a warm tingly feeling. The longer this feeling stays with me, the more filled with love I become. The other I call the Presence of Jesus, which was the feeling of wave after wave of Love, filling my whole being. I realize the Father, Spirit, and Son are one, but the feelings were so different and to distinguish between them, I labeled them as such.

I felt the feeling of the Presence of Jesus within me every day, starting with the time I experienced the lesson on submission, and then, after several months, it was gone. Confusion set in.

Was this really the manifestation of God's Presence within me? My imagination? The devil? I had entered the change of life. Was this all part of premenopausal symptoms? Was all this just a series of coincidences? Why did I feel this Presence of the Holy Spirit when I was praying, when I went to Church? Why did it fill me with such love? If this was a hot flash would it occur at such set times?

This was the time I had to sort everything out in my own mind. To wonder. To question. To pray. To turn toward God for the answers. To grow in my faith and trust. No person that I asked had the answers. No one had felt anything I was feeling. Alone. I never felt so alone before.

God does not leave us alone.

In the Catholic bookstore I looked for another book by Thomas Keating. Next to his books, I saw a book by

Song of Hope

St. Teresa of Avila. Keating had mentioned that she was
a contemplative. Wondering if she wrote on the subject
I pulled the book, The Book of Her Life, off the shelf. I
opened the book to a page at random and started reading
a description of what I was experiencing, the lack of
energy, the blank mind except for words of praise, the
feeling of wave after wave of love, the confusion. Here
was someone who understood! I flipped to another page.
Another description. Contemplative prayer was what
St. Teresa wrote about!

Since then I have read many books on contemplative
prayer. It is a moment, and a life style, of being constantly
aware of God's Presence in the present moment. There
is active and passive contemplative prayer. Active is living
for God, starting the day by giving everything you think,
say, or do, to God. Living the day by sharing the Love
He has given you, passing it on to others. A contemplative
takes the time to BE in the Presence of God, to sit, be still,
and listen. The act of quieting yourself is called Centering
Prayer. This is as much as a person can do on their own.
Actually, this is all from God, for He is the one that gives
you the desire in the first place.

Passive contemplative prayer takes a person
beyond his/herself. Resting in the spirit is a form of
passive contemplative prayer. It is not something we
can bring on ourselves.

When resting in the spirit, at first I can feel the
floor, hear the sounds around me, and I think thoughts
about God or talk to Him. When I go deeper, my awareness diminishes, my mind becomes more blank. I go
through the cloud of forgetfulness and enter the cloud of

unknowing.

Knowledge cannot get me to this point. Words cannot describe it. Sometimes it is like sleep, but it's different. One way I can tell that I've just experienced this, is that upon becoming aware, I feel as if I am lying within my lover's arms. I am very happy and content, with no reason to be.

Another way I know I have experienced this, is because I have changed so much. Suddenly I understood the scriptures. I was filled with such peace, such happiness, such love. And this love overflows to those around me, including those who have hurt me. Even my body language changes, and those with whom I have always been uncomfortable with, I am totally at ease with, and they with me.

I changed in that I wanted to love God and live my life for Him.

Sometimes in this state of deep passive contemplative prayer, God reveals the lesson He is instilling within me so that I become aware of learning it.

One night when I went to bed I thought about the Catholic belief that the substance of the bread and wine was transformed into the Body and Blood of Jesus during the consecration of Mass. I believed this because this is the teaching of my religion. I believed this because of the stories handed down of miracles of blood coming from the Host. I believed - but I didn't really believe. That night I prayed, "Please remove my unbelief." I went to sleep feeling the Presence of the Holy Spirit about me.

During the night I was awakened by a bright light. I was encased in a box of light. I said, "Lord, I do not know what this means, but I am your servant. You are the potter. I am the clay. Mold me. Meld me." And went back to sleep.

The next day I didn't think of this bright light right away. When I went to turn on my computer, I remembered it, and the insight jolted me. I cannot really explain how I felt, but I realized that I was a different person! I realized that I had absolute Faith that the bread and wine was transformed into the Body and Blood of Jesus. From that moment on I no longer questioned whether what I was feeling were manifestations of the Presence of God in my life. I KNEW! The Faith I now have is beyond all reason, beyond all logic, beyond all description.

Later, when I read the Desert Fathers' description of infused Faith and the Light of the Holy Spirit that brings Knowledge, I knew and understood exactly what they meant. God is everywhere. He is with us always, twenty-four hours a day. He invites us to come to His house to receive the Eucharist, for there we can receive Jesus as our strength and nourishment for the day. With the realization that God was indeed everywhere, He taught me the value of the Eucharist in my daily life. This is God's Gift to us. His greatest Gift. As we take Him into ourselves, He becomes our strength, our nourishment, the grace we need to live our lives in the world. Our body becomes His temple and through us He is brought forth into the world.

Lord, Jesus Christ, Son of the Living God, instill within me Your Holy Spirit and enable me to submit to You, for I want to be the best player on Your Team.

CHARISMATIC RETREAT

I went on my first Charismatic Retreat six weeks after I was Baptized in the Holy Spirit.

What is Charismatic and what is this Baptism of the Holy Spirit? We receive the Holy Spirit when we are baptized. This is when our relationship with God begins. God the Father is within us. Jesus is within us. The Holy Spirit is within us. The Trinity dwells within all baptized Christians. It is a fire within us.

Our baptismal vows are renewed when we are confirmed. We look at our Faith more seriously and make a commitment to follow the precepts of our religion. We promise to become soldiers of Christ.

Often, we let this fire die down within us. At least I did. The fire is still there, a smoldering ember. I went to Mass because it was the thing to do on Sundays. I said my prayers before meals and sometimes I remembered to think of God at bedtime. I did start each day giving my thoughts, words and deeds to Him, but usually did not give God another thought during the day, except when I thanked Him for the beauty around me. In times of crisis, I turned to Him.

Baptism of the Holy Spirit is when this fire is fanned into flame. We become an active participant in our Faith. The Gifts of the Holy Spirit pour into and out of us. These Gifts can be nurtured and manifested by

21

Song of Hope

joining Charismatic or contemplative prayer groups, or saying the rosary. In these prayer groups the gifts are taught and nourished, and they grow. From the prayer groups our spiritual life spreads as we attend daily Mass, read scripture and increase our private prayer life. We begin to volunteer our time to social services such as working in the Free Meals program, visiting the sick and the elderly, volunteering to lead, to teach.

If our Gifts remain only within the prayer group, they die. Jesus wants us to feel His love, but He wants us to love Him in return. He is in the poor, the lonely, the forsaken. We cannot just go to a prayer group to feel cozy and comfy. We must have our gifts nourished there, but then we must take them to the world around us.

Likewise, we cannot go out into the world of service and forsake our prayer life. We need the group to continue to pray for our ministry, confirm us, and refresh us.

I try to say the rosary daily. When attending a Charismatic Mass, I lift my arms high in praise to the Lord. He has healed me. I can move. I can feel. I have emotions once again. I will gladly dance to the Lord, for He has given me movement. He has filled my heart with joy. He has also drawn me into deep contemplative prayer and given me a great love for Himself.

Why do more healings take place during a healing or Charismatic Mass? For one thing, you have a priest whom God is using as His instrument to have His love flow through him into another. For another thing, you have a room filled with people on fire for love of God. All this love is flowing from them, uniting, and becoming very powerful as it encompasses the room, manifesting itself in people Resting in the Spirit, being healed physically and spiritually, being hugged by God. God wants us to feel His love. He wants us to be on fire for love of Him. He wants us to take this love to the whole world. For God is Love.

Father John Campoli was the main speaker at the Charismatic Retreat that I went on. He was the priest who had prayed over me six weeks before. At that time I had not fallen.

At the retreat I fell for the first time. As Father prayed over me, I prayed that all my barriers be removed. Suddenly I felt as light as a feather. I could not have resisted in any way. There was no push. I just became as a feather and backwards I went. I did not faint. I felt hands catch me. I felt the floor. I heard the sounds around me. I was aware of everything and of God. I could not move. I did not try to speak. When this feeling released me, I returned to my bench.

At this retreat, many things happened to me to draw me into a deeper relationship with Jesus. Falling for the first time was one.

I felt Jesus come into me and wave after wave of His love flow through me. The words spoken into my thoughts were, "Kathy, you know how hurt you feel when people do not trust you. That is how I feel when you don't trust me."

Many people had personal mystical experiences at this retreat, as Jesus drew them closer to Himself. A friend, looking into the face of the crucified Jesus, saw tears running down his cheeks. As Father Campoli knelt after the consecration, she saw Jesus descend from above and enter Father. During communion, she saw flesh hang from the host and blood drip from the chalice.

Later, a woman with the Gift of the Prophetic word, a stranger to us, cried out, "My children. My children. Those who saw me weep have not given all your pain to me. Give me your pain." With these words, she confirmed the experiences of my friend, a person suffering from extreme back pain.

At Charismatic gatherings the gifts of the Holy Spirit flow. I met an interesting person at this retreat who gave me my first prophetic word. Prophetic words can take the form such as a person speaking as if Jesus was speaking from her, like the woman I just described in the above paragraph.

The prophetic messages that have been given to me have taken the form of a description of my relation-ship with God. I have located almost all of them in scripture, so I do not believe that these messages apply only to me, but apply to all people who begin to take to heart God's Word.

After the break of the morning session of the first day, just before Father Campoli began speaking, the per-son sitting next to me got up and left. Her place was immediately filled with a young woman. At a conference, people normally sit in the same chairs meeting after meeting and so I was surprised at this. The young woman sitting next to me was wearing a beautiful blue/green medallion that matched her outfit. I complimented her on it just as Father began to speak. Even though he was speaking, she continued to whisper to me, "I am a lay contemplative with the Benedictine Order at Big Sur."

I had been wondering if what I was experiencing was contemplative prayer. Here was a person who sat down next to me saying she was a contemplative. I did not think it was coincidence. I quickly asked if I could sit with her for lunch.

During lunch I couldn't get my questions asked, so I invited her to walk around the grounds with me. I told her some of my experiences. She said she didn't feel the Holy Spirit the same way, but each feels as God permits.

Suddenly she said, "I feel the Presence of the Holy Spirit. Do you?"

"Yes, I do," I answered as His Presence came over me.

"Are you getting a message?" she asked.

"No. Other people usually get the message and give them to me. Are you getting a message?"

"I'm not in the listening mode." She apparently got into this mode for she began speaking, holding the stance of someone listening and then repeating what they heard. She said, "My children. I have planted you firmly and deeply in the ground. You will grow taller than the tallest Cedar of Lebanon, higher than the highest palm." She looked at me. "That means you won't be a little bush." She continued her listening. "This is your prayer. Say it often. Put on the armor of Christ. Clothe yourself with the helmet of salvation, the breastplate of righteousness..."

"That's my prayer!" I interrupted. "I was given that protection-prayer not too long ago."

"Say it. Say it often. Say it continuously. That is your prayer."

I thanked her and she said she didn't mind being God's tool, even if it meant being a telephone.

I am not a scripture scholar. It took me three years,

and then, there it was before me. Psalm 92:13-16.

I do not know who put into words the protection-prayer. "Father, pour forth your blood upon me. Please send forth your angels and saints to watch over, bless, guide and protect us, especially St. Michael the archangel, St. Raphael the healing angel. Mary, our Mother, please intercede for me. Father, please fill me and surround me with your Holy Spirit. Father, please place the protective hedge of thorns of your son, Jesus, around me, so that every thought, word and deed are filtered through Jesus. Father, by the cross of Jesus, the blood of Jesus, the name of Jesus, lead me and protect me. Father, please clothe me in the armor of Christ, as I put on the helmet of salvation, the breastplate of righteousness, truth as a belt around my waist, zeal to propagate the gospel of peace as my footgear, as I take up the sword of the spirit and the shield of faith. Amen."

Father, you have planted me in the house of the Lord through my Baptism. You are my rock holding me firm. Help me to grow and be fruitful.

POUR OUT YOUR SPIRIT

When you are Baptized in the Spirit, the date becomes ingrained in your memory, and the person through whom you received this Gift becomes special in your life. Whenever Father John Campoli, who is from New Jersey, was near my area I went to his services as often as I could.

I was invited by the "Friday Night with Jesus Ministries" to photograph and write about the Parish Mission at Marysville, California. Fr. John Campoli and Deacon Bill Warren were the speakers. The mission started Friday evening with a Mass for Healing. We received the Sacrament of the sick and prayed for the inflowing of the Holy Spirit into our lives. The mission went all day Saturday, with a Youth Mass that evening. We were asked to accept Jesus into our lives. Sunday included a special time for individual prayer for healing.

I listened to Father Campoli: "God has miracle upon miracle to pour into our lives. Open your eyes and see His Presence in Your life."

I have heard Father Campoli over thirty times. I like what he says and how he says it. He expresses the spirituality for which I have hungered all my life. Each time I hear him is like a fresh new experience. That's because he talks about God revealing Himself to us. I knew that what he said about God having a miracle for each one there that night was true.

27

Song of Hope

Before the Holy Spirit became more active in my life, I considered myself a "normal" Catholic. I went to Church on Sunday because I had to. Confession? Didn't the church do away with that Sacrament? Praying? Oh, I thought of Him when things were going very badly for me. Miracles? IF they happened at all, they happened to other people. I hoped in God, I believed in God, I loved God - but I did not trust Him.

I lived in much pain, which I considered part of growing old. I was very unhappy and I savored remembering how others had stabbed me in the back. I thought God loved others, but not me. I could easily pray for others, but not for myself.

When Father Campoli came to our area, what he said sounded very nice. If only God would do such nice things to me! But would He? He only does that for Holy people — priests, nuns, people who spent their days in prayer. I knew that wouldn't happen to me.

In Marysville I listened to Fr. Campoli saying, "God loves us as no other person on Earth does or can. Think! He died for me — not just for the whole world collectively, but for me, personally as well. Too many people think, He died for the world, but not for me."

Father Campoli said, "God wants your life. He wants to give you the Gift of Salvation. And once you accept this gift, you'll never be the same person again. You become a tool, an instrument with Jesus by accepting Jesus Christ as your personal Lord and Savior. Then the Holy Spirit is poured into your life."

I had heard Deacon Bill Warren only once before. The two speakers complemented each other. Words of hope. Words of faith. Words of love. Deacon Bill said,

"Once God touches one area of our lives, He touches all areas of our lives. He heals us physically. He calls us to a closer relationship with Him. He heals our relationships."

Deacon Bill had been healed of cancer. Fr. Campoli had a blocked artery in his heart and a new artery grew. Since the time I went to my first Mass for Healing, God has taken away all my pain and He has begun healing me of painful memories.

Fr. Campoli said, "Forgiveness is the biggest obstacle to leading a Christian life. We love to complain. We do not forgive as we should, but God can forgive for us. Jesus died for the murderer as much as He did for us."

I had been hurt. I was not going to forgive. I, Kathy Moore, had a catty reply all planned if this person ever came to me to apologize. I told God if He wanted me to forgive, He would have to help me, for I could not do it on my own. One day during Mass, I felt the Holy Spirit come over me and stay with me. The longer I have this feeling, the more love I feel. This person came to me during the sign of peace and asked for my forgiveness. The love that flowed out of me was not from me, Kathy Moore. It was beyond anything I was capable of. Beyond my humanness.

Deacon Bill said, "The Holy Spirit heals our soul, our spirit, our relationships with one another."

As I listened to Fr. Campoli and Deacon Bill Warren I realized so many of the things they said had indeed come true in my life. My life. Not someone else's life. Not the other person's life. My life. And if it can happen to me, it can happen to you.

`Deacon Bill Warren said, "We are the vessels and the Holy Spirit fills us. Trouble is, we're cracked.

Song of Hope

Cracked pots. God's light shines through the cracks in the pot — shines through our weaknesses so His strength shines forth."

These two men give witness to God in their lives. They give witness to the truths as recorded in Scripture. Each time I hear them it is fresh and exciting. That is how God's Word is. The Holy Spirit opens our eyes to the wonders and mysteries of God. Each day becomes a new adventure as we wonder what God is going to reveal to us that day as we become more aware of God's constant Presence in every aspect of our lives. Fr. Campoli said, "We are familiar with the translation of God's name as 'I am'. Another translation reads, 'You will find me in the things that happen'".

Father Campoli said, "Watch for the fruits of the Holy Spirit pouring into your life." I have never been happier, more at peace, more in love in my life.

We have the Holy Spirit within us from our Baptism, and from our Confirmation. It is an ember sitting within us, waiting to be blown into flame. God uses certain people to help blow the Holy Spirit within us into flame. These people are anywhere, everywhere — anyone who turns us toward wanting Jesus Christ as Our Lord and Savior in our lives. In some people, God manifests this Gift in more powerful ways. A person who has been granted the Gift of Healing is one of these.

Do not limit the Gift of Healing to only physical healing. God will work in the power of His Spirit in you and through you in the way He knows best. The Gift of the Spirit you may receive may not be physical healing, but rather the strength and the peace within to bear your pain. The Gift might be wisdom or counsel, knowledge or understanding, so that you can help others around you. The Gift poured out into you might be the Gift of Healing or prophecy, teaching, or exhortation. It might be the Gift to accept help offered to you.

Come and claim the miracle God has for you. Miracles aren't for other people. They're for each one of us. They are Gifts God wants to give us. Come.

I accept Jesus Christ as Lord and Savior of my life.
Fan Your Spirit into flame within me.
Pour Your Spirit into my life.

Song of Hope

FEAR!!

Not long ago I climbed a fully extended ladder and
painted the apex of our church. I wish someone had
taken my picture. I used to be afraid of heights. I know
what fear is. Paralyzing fear that makes you freeze to
the spot, unable to move.

I wasn't born with this fear. I lived in the tops of
trees as a child. If my mother went looking for me, she
looked up. It wasn't until I was in college that I saw that
my mother was petrified of heights and I marveled that
she had not given me this fear.

One day I was climbing to some caves. The climb
was straight up using hand holds and toe holds. I was
about 12 to 15 feet up when my boyfriend saw what I
was doing. "Kathy," he yelled. "Look down."

The rule for climbing is never look down. You
don't get in a car thinking I'm going to crash. You don't
climb thinking I'm going to fall. "Ted" continued, "Look
down. Look what would happen if you fell." For the
first time I saw all these rocks down below me. For the
first time in my life, I knew what fear was. I could not
move. I could not move for at least 45 minutes. I was
frozen to that rock wall. When I was finally down, that
was the end of that relationship. I could never forgive
him for instilling in me such a fear.

From then on, whenever I was in a steep place in

32

the mountains, his words would come back and haunt me. I could not enjoy the beauty around me. Gone was the excitement, the glorious feeling of being on top of the world. Instead I would sit down and cry and shake. My climbing companions thought I was mad at them. I couldn't bring myself to even talk about this fear. I was also very ashamed of it. I would lash out at my companions saying, "Leave me alone," and thus break off that relationship.

Shortly after I was Baptized in the Spirit, when I felt the Presence of the Holy Spirit engulf me with love, I had a choice. I could turn toward God, accept Jesus Christ into my life, or I could continue living like I was. I was not happy, but at least I was comfortable in my unhappiness. I knew what that was all about. To say yes to God instilled within me a fear, a paralyzing fear, not unlike the fear of heights I had acquired. What would He ask of me? What would He expect of me? Where would my future go with Him? What would He ask me to give up?

I was standing next to a statue of the Virgin Mary with a friend and we talked about this fear. I told her about my mother's fear. I still did not talk about my own. My family had gone to Disneyland and we talked Mom into going on the gondola ride. She tried to get out of it, but once going up the long flight of steps, there was no turning back. I leaned out exclaiming, "Look at the mermaid. Look at this. Look at that." Mom always answered, "hummm." Then I turned and looked at her. She was frozen, staring straight ahead, but forcing herself to answer calmly. It was the first time I had seen her fear. And I was in college! Another time we went to the Tetons and rode to the top in a huge gondola. This gondola held at least 30 people and so this ride didn't bother Mom. I was the first one off and ran to the top of the mountain. What a view! What a feeling! I hurried back to get Mom. She was the last one off. Just as she went to step out of the gondola the wind blew. A two inch gap showed between the gondola and the platform. Looking through that two inch gap revealed the shear drop of 5,000 feet. I saw the fear cross my mother's face for only an instant. She calmly said, "I think I'll enjoy the view from here." I wanted her to enjoy what I had. I held out my hand and helped her across.

My friend held out her hand to offer help and support on my acceptance of Jesus into my life but I couldn't take it. I was literally terrified to do so. So she turned and let me be with my thoughts. I was alone with Virgin Mary and so I talked to her. I felt her say to me, "Remember how you felt on the mountain top — the joy, the peace, the contentment? That's how it will be with God."

I wondered, "I have to make a living and I can't do that on a mountain top."

Again I felt her say in my thoughts, "God will provide."

"Take my hand and help me across?" and I held out my hand symbolically for I needed Mary's help to go to Jesus. Soon my friend returned and this time I held out my hand to her. She took it and we prayed together.

God began to take away my fears. My fear of heights stemmed from an incident that I remembered. This hurt produced a fear within me. This fear made me lash out and ruin friendships. First I had to give the incident to God. The incident and the memory of it - -

all for the Greater Honor and Glory of His Name, and I
gave the hurt I experienced to Jesus, entrusting to His
love.

Then I asked God to forgive "Ted". I asked Him
to help me forgive him, for I couldn't do it on my own.

I asked Jesus to heal this hurt. To comfort me. To
take away the pain, the bitterness.

Lastly, to really give the problem, the pain to Jesus,
was the hardest to learn, hardest to do. It was easy to
say: "Give it to Jesus!" But to really do it, was almost
impossible. I would give it to Jesus but every time He
would begin to take it, I would grab on tight and not let
go. I was familiar with this hurt. I relished feeling sorry
for myself. I relished blaming "Ted" for this fear I had.
I had to WANT genuinely to change and ask God to help
me get rid of this hurt. I finally said, "If it's Your will
that I experience such a hurt again, OK. If it's Your will
that I do Your work on a mountain top, I will trust that
You will take away this fear of heights. If it's Your will
that I continue to live with this fear of heights, so be it. I
want to do Your will."

God does not will that we suffer. He does not will
that we have fears and pain. He wills us all to be whole,
to Glorify Him in our wholeness. God loves us and, as
we accept this love, He takes away all fear. But if for
reasons only He knows, He does not step in and heal us,
accept this. He might want our faith and trust to grow
more. The devil also tries to step in and pull us away
from God with thoughts of fear, to take away this faith
and trust we are trying to receive from God.

I know that when I think that God will not take
away this fear, and then I say, OK, I accept this fear, this

pain," — it's taken away.

I did not experience a flash of light or anything else connected with this fear. I have no idea when I realized I was no longer afraid of heights. Maybe when I realized so many of my other fears were gone. But when I had a chance to go up in a hot air balloon, I didn't think twice. I got in and enjoyed every minute of it.

The messages from Mary at Medjugorje are always, "Pray. Fast. Be converted." Being converted means to turn toward God, but not just once. Daily. Give Him yourself each day. Give Jesus your hurts for the day, the stabs in the back that you've just received. Give Him your problems. Let Him handle them. Then you become free to smile, to enjoy life, to climb mountains and enjoy the view, to be your whole self, without fears. To be all you can be.

Jesus, I give You my hurts, I give You my fears,
I give You my pain.
Forgive all who have hurt me
and help me forgive them.
Please heal me of my hatred, my bitterness, my fears
that these hurts have grown into. Let my smile be
Your smile toward the whole world.

BE STILL AND KNOW THAT I AM GOD

All people, everyone, everywhere, are called into contemplative prayer. It is not just for the few, not just for those with the nature of being quiet, not just for those in cloisters living in silence. We all know the story of Mary and Martha. As Mary sat in stillness at Jesus' feet, Jesus said that she had chosen the better portion. We all have to be Marthas as we live in this world. She was the active contemplative. Her heart and soul, her day, her work, her thoughts were directed toward Jesus. But we are all called to sit quietly at Jesus' feet and slip into passive contemplation, to sit in stillness and hear His voice. Contemplation is the prayer of listening. It is giving Jesus the time to talk to us. It is the prayer of love, in which we give Him our whole being, our whole attention.

The first time I experienced the first level of passive contemplative prayer was when I Rested in the Spirit. I did not fall but went to my pew, the church disappeared, and I became alone with God. At a later time, when I experienced falling for the first time, all energy left me and I felt as a feather. I could not stand so over I went, straight backwards. I felt hands catch me, felt the floor, heard the noise around me. The feeling was the same. The church disappeared and I felt alone with God. I felt engulfed in His love. A great peace entered me. I didn't want to move. I didn't want this feeling to go away. Why

37

should I? I was resting in the arms of Jesus, resting in His love, and I knew it. Why would I want to pull myself away?

Jesus releases us back into our world. I became aware of my surroundings, slightly embarrassed that I was lying on the church floor. But the world had me again, fearful of what others thought of me.

I realized I had a wrong concept of God in thinking of Him as a figure in the sky that does not care about the creatures He has made. I saw that He is right here, within us and around us, and He loves us. I thought myself unworthy of this love, but there I was, feeling engulfed in it. Why shouldn't He love me? Don't we love our own children? Do we think them unworthy of our love, or desire that they should think this? To think that Jesus died for me, and then me not accepting this love because I considered myself too unworthy, how would this make Him feel? He died for my sins, my faults, not for my goodness, my talents. Jesus wants to love us, wants to heal us, wants us to come to Him, to trust Him, believe in Him, put our hope in Him, to love Him in return.

These convictions came to me slowly, over months of "listening." God opened my eyes and ears to what I had been taught during the priests' homilies all my life.

I know that I could not duplicate the experience of Resting in the Spirit in my wildest imagination. I know it was from God. Yet I wasn't sure. "What happened to me?" I asked. Someone told me I was feeling the Presence of the Holy Spirit and I was invited to a Charismatic prayer group. I learned about the gifts of the Holy Spirit. I read scripture and books. I was introduced to worship and praise music that lifted my soul into prayer.

Organizations such as "Friday Night with Jesus" brought outstanding Catholic speakers to our area and I learned more about my religion and how God was working in many lives.

God drew me into passive contemplative prayer at home. As time passed, I realized that God healed me during these experiences. Healed me physically, and spiritually. He took away all my pain and began to take away the hurt in my memories. He also drew me closer to Him.

I read the book by St. Teresa of Avila, <u>The Book of Her Life</u>. I realized contemplative prayer and the way God changes a person as He calls them to Himself were the same as how the Charismatics were describing the workings of the Holy Spirit within a person. Sitting quietly and feeling God's love is wonderful, but what is happening to us? Very seldom are we given visions or even a voice instructing us through our thoughts. How do we know our time isn't wasted? We know by the way our lives change.

Slowly we are drawn deep into God's love, and that means conversion, changing our lives, willing to die to our selfish ways, to turn away from the disordered materialism of the world, willing to love our neighbor, willing to go through the refiner's fire of persecution and suffering.

We can stop at any time, say this is too much for me at this time and God will wait. Or we can be willing to go deeper into His love. At some point we have to turn off the music, sit in stillness, quiet our mind, and give ourselves totally to God, give Him a chance to speak to us, and to listen.

Song of Hope

To experience a personal relationship with Jesus
is a Gift from God. To know that this experience is from
God, is another Gift. To understand the experience is yet
another Gift. These gifts may be given simultaneously
or years apart. To Rest in the Spirit, to slip into passive
contemplative prayer, is a Gift from God. I realize now
that I have experienced this same feeling many times, only
it was a fleeting feeling. Alone with God after receiving
communion. Alone with God in a shady mountain glen.
Alone with God before a majestic sunset. Each time, with
this Grace, I moved a step closer in my love with God,
in my faith in Him until finally the time was right. Using
the healing priest as His tool, God stirred into flame this
love, this faith. He called me by name and I became His.

We can all recognize these moments of contemplative prayer when we are aware of God's Presence,
when we are aware of God within us and around us, and
we become still within that Presence. Sometimes we are
given a feeling to accompany this awareness of His
Presence, a feeling of joy, or peace, or calm, or love that
springs from deep within us.

To live a contemplative life is being aware of
God's Presence at all times, to see God in all things, to
live within His Presence within the moment and accept
that moment as being His will.

A person must go through the actions of reading
scripture, praying, attending Mass, helping others around
them. All these things help us establish a relationship
with God. It is like getting acquainted with our future
spouse. We spend time with them, we think about them,
we learn everything we can about them. As our relationship grows, we become comfortable just sitting side

by side, just being aware of each other's presence. We can feel the love for each other flow from one to the other.

St. Teresa of Avila compared it to bringing water to a garden. In the beginning we have to carry the water in buckets in order to get the things to grow. Later we build an aqueduct and the water comes to the garden with less effort on our part, and finally God supplies all the water necessary by rain and springs and the plants flourish.

It's like a husband and wife in the kitchen together, the woman at the sink doing dishes, the man at the table paying bills. Suddenly the distance between them is too great. The woman reaches for a towel to dry her hands, the man, with the same feeling, rises from his chair and in a moment is at her side. They just stand there, holding one another close, not saying a word, not moving, as the love flows all around them. Their whole being swells with this love and they know that any words would be inadequate to express it. They could hold each other all night and all their caresses would not convey adequately this love.

This really falls short in describing feeling God's love, but it is something most can relate to. We can do dishes, clean, work, bring home the pay check, to show our love for our spouse, but we still need that moment of silence, of holding each other close.

We can pray, we can read scripture, we can visit the sick and feed the poor, but we still need that moment of silence, of just sitting in the Presence of God, of giving Him our complete attention by simply giving Him our time. Be still and know that He is God.

Song of Hope

Father, our creator,
help me take the time to smell the roses
and be aware of Your Presence within that moment!

GOD IS LOVE

We say that we love God. We are taught "God is Love" and that He loves us unconditionally. We all have our ideas of what "love" means by our own experiences in our lives.

My understanding of love: When I talk about the most loving situations in my life, I think of sitting on my mother's lap, being held by her, of running to her with an owie to be kissed. I think of the love I felt during my courtship days, how my heart beat faster when I was around this fellow, and how my face had this glow of happiness. I think of the love I felt when I first saw my first born son as the doctor held him out to me. I think of the comfortable love I feel when I walk around my property with my youngest son, pointing out the various flowers that are blooming.

Our ideas of love are also our ideas of God. This could be an error and barrier to understanding and accepting God's love.

I did not have a happy marriage. That is not very conducive to self-esteem. When the one closest to you doesn't like you, it is hard to imagine anyone else liking you, and that includes God.

Since I became Baptized in the Spirit, people in various situations and illnesses came into my life to be added to my prayers. I could pray for all sorts of things

43

and for other people, but found it very hard to pray for myself. Prayers concerning relationships with people have not always gone the way I asked. Yet, my prayers for a better relationship with God have been answered in very awesome ways. I felt like a door to door solicitor for funds to build the community swimming pool. I knock on one door and I'm given a thousand dollars for myself for asking! The swimming pool fund goes empty, but I am rewarded! That's how I have felt with many of my prayers. The people go unhealed, but I am rewarded with God's love showered upon me!

I felt that I was praying wrongly but a retreat master reassured me: "God gives you what you need. You needed love, more than the others needed to be healed."

One day I realized that although I gave my problems to God, I didn't let go of them. I had the same ones the very next day. I realized that I had to give all of me to God — my problems, my achievements, my sins, my goodness, my ignorance, my skills, my ineptness, my talents — all to God. I gave myself to Him the only way I knew how; I gave Him my time.

It was a beautiful July Sunday. It was a major turning point in my relationship with God. All I have written thus far can be labeled phase one. Phase one covered God's showering His Love upon me. This beautiful July Sunday marked the beginning of phase two.

I wanted to take a hike into the mountains. Instead I came home from church and shut myself up in my room. I shut away the world, I shut away the beauty, I closed my eyes and shut away my room. Nothing happened that I was aware of. I didn't feel God's Presence nor His love. I even felt the lack of His Presence — an abandoned feeling.

I prayed, "Lord, if there are any barriers to my being completely filled with your Holy Spirit, please bring them to my mind, so that they can be removed."

A lesson I was taught stemmed from this prayer and continued on through phase two. Our capacity to love God is limited by the barriers within us allowing us to accept His love. God gives us His love to love Himself. We have to be open to receive this love.

As our barriers are eliminated we are able to accept more of God's love for us and thus love Him more.

As our barriers are eliminated the more we become one with God. The biggest obstacle is our own self and all which makes up our false self; our selfishness, our independence, our stubbornness. Even our good qualities, talents and virtues, give us the feeling that we can do everything by ourselves, that we don't need God. Our self becomes an idol.

As our barriers are eliminated, God's love over-flows from us to other people in mercy, compassion and love. We are freed from selfishness and become selfless. We exchange our independence for dependence upon God. We are freed from stubbornness and become pliable under His direction. The more we do so, the more of God's love we will receive and, the more we love Him.

The full realization of all of His love will come upon our death, when self is no longer disordered and thus no longer a barrier.

Thursday morning after this Sunday of choosing to give myself totally to God, I awoke feeling the Presence of the Holy Spirit. Usually it is a passing feeling, like

Song of Hope

"Good morning." But this day it stayed and the longer it stayed, the more the feeling of love grew within me. By the time I was dressed, left the bathroom and headed for the kitchen, I was ready to burst with this love within me. I had praise music on and it was rising to a crescendo.

I exclaimed out loud, even though alone in the house, "What Love! If everyone could feel this Love, there would be no more wars! No more spousal abuse! No more child abuse!"

I stepped into the kitchen and a shaft of light came down and I was engulfed in Love, saturated with Love. It flowed through me and around me, penetrating the very marrow of my bones. My heart felt a pain go into it, making me cry out, yet I did not want the pain to stop.

All was over within seconds.

Thoughts flowed through me: "God loves me! He loves me in my kitchen! He loves me in my old clothes! He loves me whether I'm rich or poor!"

Some people expressed the opinion if I had a true experience from God I would be flat on my face with ecstacy; but these thoughts <u>were</u> from God. They were removing barriers to accepting God's love for me.

A counselor once suggested that perhaps my husband didn't love me because I kept a messy house. We have all heard the expression, "Cleanliness is next to Godliness." How could God love me if I wasn't a good housekeeper? Yet God loved me in my kitchen, the messiest room in the house!

Someone else surmised, "Perhaps your husband doesn't love you because you never dress up for him." Here I was in my old clothes, yet God loved me.

We have heard that God blesses those He favors

with prosperity. I surely was not economically prosperous, therefore, I must not be in His favor.

God gave me a tremendous hug in my kitchen to show me His Love and to bring to my mind barriers that limited my accepting this love. Once they were brought to my mind, I could remove them. I had to want to remove them. I had to recognize that God would help me remove them.

I will never forget this soaking of love I received and it helped me through the days that followed during which I was shown my sins. St. Teresa wrote that often before a severe trial she received a great Gift of God's love. I received this great soaking of God's Love before my great trial and it helped me through those days.

As God showers His Love upon us, we realize we are not worthy of any of this Love. Yet He loves us. We realize we are nothing. All the talents that we have come from Him. The fact that we are breathing and alive is from Him. We are just human beings. He is God. And He loves us! He looks at us, sees us in our sinfulness, in our weakness, and He loves us all the same. Jesus did not die on the cross because of our goodness or talents. He died for us in our sinfulness. This is how much He loves us all; for God is Love.

Human love for God is like a drop of water. His Love given to me for Himself is like the ocean. It fills me and spills to everyone around me.

Eternal Father, remove my barriers so that I may become completely filled with Your Love.

HAVE MERCY UPON ME, A SINNER

God showed me my sins.

If anyone has ever experienced such a thing, these five words are sufficient. I need not say another word. They will know what I have been through.

It is a completely humbling experience, but I write about it to dispel fears some people have. Some people do not want to go into a deeper relationship with God for they have heard of this purging that one has to go through and they back off. Yes, it is a painful process, a humbling experience. So is childbirth. And the pain and the nakedness is forgotten once it is over. The Joy, the Peace, the Love which permeates you afterwards is indescribable.

God showed me my sins. It took me months to understand what He showed me, for I was more aware of my feelings than the lessons to be learned. He did not say, "Kathy, at the age of 10 you lied to your mother. At the age of 12 you..." No. He showed me my propensity to sin.

This was in my mind; but it was the only thing I could think of — all day long. Few other thoughts entered my mind. I could not turn and distract myself. I also did not feel God's Presence during this time. I felt completely abandoned by everyone. I had no one to turn to for help. Actually, I have no idea what I would have said to anyone available. I did not know this was a normal reaction.

God showed me my sins. He showed me that I had the propensity to murder, to rape, to molest. I was no different than any person in prison save for one thing — I did not do it YET.

These thoughts brought me low. How could God love me if I were such a person? I saw myself as absolute filth. Unlovable by mankind and by God. "Yet", I argued back, "God loves me! I know He loves me! He loved me in the kitchen!"

The memory of His love for me in the kitchen I hung onto as I felt at the brink of despair.

"Look at all He has given me — all the beauty around me, my sons, my family, my friends, my home! He loves me! I know He loves me!"

I argued all day long. First, how horrible I was. Then my defense. This went on for days!

The second day the battle lessened and I could think of other things. The third day I was at peace. The fourth day He showed me another sin.

This went on and on. Twelve days for sure. Maybe three weeks. I lost track of time.

I was shown that within me was a great mass of hate and bitterness and fear. I had a deep hatred for all authority. And it was from this hatred that my sins came. From this hatred came my propensity to murder. From this hatred came other sins of anger, of resentment, of back-biting, of gossiping, of ruining other people's reputations.

I saw myself as despicable, unlikable, horrid, worse than mud. My only argument against such negative thoughts was the one thought, the one reassurance,

49

Song of Hope

"God loves me!" I clung to that one hope as I was pelted with negative thoughts against myself.

My nerves became raw. I felt exhausted. What more could I say to rid myself of such negative thoughts? I was fighting for my life, my self esteem, my reason for living and being.

My eyes fell on the crucifix. It was there for me all the time, yet I never once looked at it. As I fastened my eyes on the figure of Jesus, I exclaimed, "There! There! That is how much God loves me!" Even though I was alone in the house, I shouted this out loud.

That reality taught me all my life — that God loves me so much He sent His only Son to Earth to die for me, that Jesus died for me, forgiving and removing my sins — that conviction went from my head, to my heart, my soul, into the very marrow of my bones.

As I stood there and felt this reality soak into me, a complete peace came over me.

My ordeal was over. God won another victory!

Some people ask, why have that crucifix in church? He is alive, risen and with us. Yes, He is; but the crucifix reminds us how much God loves us. If I were the only person on earth and it took the death of God's Son to save me, He would do it.

Being shown my sins took months to understand. I came to realize that my propensity to sin stemmed, in part, from hurts. Painful remarks or injustices inflicted upon me in my youth and not forgiven but maybe forgotten caused immense hatred to grow in me. For example, a chance remark from a second grade music teacher made me not only self-conscious, and destroyed my love and participation in all singing, but also poisoned my attitude to all public speaking and all authority figures. This one, unforgiven injury, seemed to have left me a broken person. I was not whole. I seemed prevented from being all I could be. I could not be a singer, nor publicly speak in front of others. I became super-sensitive to the next belittling remark. It had never dawned on me that this was a bad day for the teacher, the nun, the priest, who-ever — or myself; that people change, including myself and all who hurt me. Unforgivingness is an infection which grows, if not treated properly.

The music teacher's remark (surely not intended to harm me) is but one example. Think of all the more devastating hurts inflicted on children by adults! The effects of humiliating a child in public (or private) can be destructive and lasting.

On our own, we cannot forgive adequately; but only through God we can. One by one, God continues to bring to my mind hurtful memories. I no longer brood or cry about them, or wallow in how unfairly I have been treated all my life. I have learned several steps to be healed of these hurts.

One, I offer the incident and the memory to God for His greater honor and glory. Two, I give the incident to Jesus to add to His healing love. Three, I ask God to forgive the persons who injured me and ask for help to forgive them. Four, I plead with God to heal the injury and the pain. And five, I give it to Jesus, for the devil tries to take away hope and trust, and to condemn me. I also say that, if God permits I be hurt in this way again, or if I am not freed of the pain or can not avoid it, I accept it.

God does not take away the memory. Good grief.

Song of Hope

I wouldn't have a memory left! He takes away the pain, the bitterness, the hate. Once I recognize the causes of my limitations and defects, they can be removed. I can be whole once again.

If God draws you into this experience, talk with someone — your pastor, your spiritual director. If you are alone, do not despair. God is in and with you. He holds you in His hand. He permits such experiences to heal and draw you closer to Himself.

Jesus Christ, Son of the Living God,
have mercy on me, a sinner!

A MOUNTAIN HIKE

One beautiful Saturday in late August I planned a mountain hike. I arrived at Taylor Lake at 6:30 a.m. The name of a lake, Big Blue, appealed to me and that was my destination. I carried my camera, a Nikon with a zoom lens, and an insulated lunch bag with a sandwich and a pint of water. I also had a fishing pole and wore a fishing vest with a few hooks and a topographical map.

When I arrived back at the lake, I asked a camper for the time. It was 6:30 p.m. I had been gone twelve hours! During that time I had not seen one other person. During those twelve hours my only thoughts were of God. In my opinion, that is humanly impossible. I have never before or since spent that long a time thinking of one subject. My thoughts normally go every which way. I think of my problems, finances, my sons, but this day was spent thinking about and giving praise and thanksgiving to God.

At approximately one o'clock I stopped and ate lunch. I was three fourths of the way up a steep ridge following a trail through rock talus. Far below me lay a mountain lake. From my vantage point I could see over the mountain ridges for a hundred miles. On the other side of the ridge was Big Blue Lake. It would take me another two hours to make it to the top. Not being in shape for this mountain hike, I was tired. My feet were

53

already blistered and I had to hike all the way back. With deep regret, I gave up my plans to reach Big Blue and turned for home.

At Twin Lake I stopped and cooled off with a swim. I am not a fisherman. Why I carried a fishing pole is beyond me. I only had two flies and I could only fling the line about three feet from me. Dragonflies were darting about everywhere. With a sudden idea, I tied a small twig to my line a few inches from the fly and it then looked like a dragonfly. I also could fling the line out further into the water. To my amazement I quickly caught two eight-inch trout. I then headed for home.

My feet were blistered. My camera and two fish increased in weight with every step I took. I wondered aloud in my talk to God if I would have to spend the night in the mountains.

Suddenly, my feet no longer hurt and my camera and my lunch bag became weightless! I couldn't get over what I was feeling - or rather, what I wasn't feeling. Was this God's thank you to me for the day? He removed all my burdens! When I reached Taylor Lake I felt refreshed!

God is everywhere. I have felt especially close to Him in the mountains. The green trees, the wild flowers, the dusty trail, the blue, clear lakes, the wind swirling and cooling, and the gorgeous view ever present before me makes it easy for me to keep God constantly in my thoughts. I have said many times, "Why go into a Church building when I can praise God in the mountains."

Not long ago a memory surfaced. I grew up in Wisconsin. My best friend down the street and I played together every week, one Saturday at my house, the next at hers. One day she refused to play at my house. I said, "I won't play with you unless you come to my house."

She said, "Fine. Don't play with me."

I gave in and went to her house. I have no idea what set her off. Whatever it was, I was free to play with her at her house, but she never again came to my house to play.

God is indeed everywhere. He teaches me the value of the Eucharist in my daily life, and in what ways I have to change. He gives me yet another lesson - the memory of the incident with my friend. God is with us at all times, but He invites us to His special house of worship at least once a week for one hour. Will we act like my friend and say, "No, You just have to be at my house; I will not come to Yours." God is indeed on the mountains. He is also within us. We are His temple. But His greatest gift to us is His Son, Jesus. Jesus is that Eucharist we receive at Communion. We take Him into ourselves. He deepens His life in us and becomes our strength, our nourishment. One with Him, we become His hands, His feet, His voice. This is our eternal Gift as the Incarnate Word is born within us and all generations again and again. We cannot give ourselves, as Jesus, without first becoming sons and daughters of God, through baptism and being nurtured with this Eucharist. We have to come into the world with Jesus' own Gifts of Love, Mercy, Compassion, Teaching, Encouragement, Prophecy, Healing.

My Eternal Father,
give me the desire to spend time with You!

PRESENCE OF GOD

God makes His Presence known to us in many ways. I no longer believe in mere coincidences. God works in our thought processes and is in every event of our lives.

I also "feel" God's presence in a physical way — I feel the Holy Spirit coming over me and filling me.

I am not describing God. I'm describing my feeling of God in terms I hope are understandable or recognizable by persons who have experienced God in similar ways.

How can I describe a feeling? I try by relating it to other feelings most people have experienced.

I have a sense of God's presence continually, in this manner:

When I was a child I liked to study in the living room. I liked being with the rest of the family. My back would be to them, the t.v. would be off, they would be quiet, reading, knitting, correcting papers. Even though I did not see them, nor hear them, I knew they were there. I could feel their presence.

If everyone was gone and I was home alone studying, my back to the living room, the feeling would be different. I knew they were not there.

A child has that feeling, running into the house from school, that mother is in the house, in a room in which she cannot be immediately seen, or not home at all.

PRESENCE OF GOD

In this manner I have a sense of God's Presence continually.

I am filled with a deep joy, peace and love. Sometimes I feel a great calm within me. I do not feel lonely or afraid. He has removed the feeling of His Presence from me, and brought it back, so that I know what it is I feel. I feel completely abandoned when I do not feel His Presence. He is always with me, but He removes the feeling of His Presence to teach me to walk in faith, to know what it is I am feeling, and to turn to Him for everything.

Many times during my trials I also feel the lack of His Presence. This is a battle I have to fight alone, to become stronger in my faith, hope, and love. It is the same as a mother letting go of the child's hand to teach them to walk alone. Mothers have to stand and watch their children fall to give them courage to try again.

St. Teresa of Avila and St. Therese of Liseaux went for long periods of time not having this great inner feeling of the Presence of God. During this time they had to walk in faith.

This sense of joy, peace, love, patience, fortitude, within a person in spite of turbulence around them, or suffering pain, or persecution, are fruits of the spirit and signs of the Presence of God. Lacking them, however, is not a sign that God is not with them.

I am also aware of God's presence when I look at the beauty around me. I hear God's voice in the birds singing, and am aware of God's presence in the delightful fragrance of a flower.

I also feel God's Presence on a more surface level. These feelings are called sensible consolations. Although

57

Song of Hope

St. Teresa of Avila and St. John of the Cross experienced such manifestations of God's Presence, they emphasized that a person should not base their faith upon these. I have to be careful so that I don't think that God has really abandoned me just because I don't sensibly feel anything. He is still with me, I just don't feel His Presence. Some people never ever feel anything. We should not go in search of these feelings, thinking, "I will believe after I experience such a thing." Genuine mystics warn against this. God is present to a person whether or not they have these feelings. Nor ought we to travel from one healing person to another for the purpose to receive these wonderful feelings. We are invited to seek true healing of mind, body, or spirit.

Sensible consolations require a great deal of discernment, for the evil one tries to counterfeit them.

People feel the Presence of the Holy Spirit or of Jesus or of Mary in different ways. When I was at Medjugorje, I felt the Presence of Mary as a tightening around my heart. I wasn't given the Knowledge of what I felt until the next day. Some people feel the Presence of the Holy Spirit in this manner. Some people smell roses and know Mary is near. With very few exceptions, the times I have felt Mary were in Church or where the rosary was being said.

How can I describe how I feel the Presence of the Holy Spirit? I feel warmth; sometimes a prickly sensation, either all over or just in my hands. The most telling sign to me is that the longer I feel this sensation, the more Love grows within me, and I am filled with a great sense of peace.

I have a wild kitty I tamed. When I pray the

Liturgy of the Hours, it comes and lies by my side. But the moment I am filled with the Holy Spirit, it jumps into my lap.

One day I was playing a computer game and also listening to "Romans" by Father James Nisbet on an audio cassette. My kitty was asleep on the couch. During a pause, I went and sat in the arm chair. I wasn't thinking about God, nor did I consider myself in a prayerful mood, when suddenly, whoosh, I felt the Holy Spirit come over me in a very strong way. Immediately I had the cat in my lap.

I often wondered if what I was feeling was really the Presence of the Holy Spirit or something to do with my heart or hormones, but the reaction of my cat confirmed, in my opinion, that it is the Holy Spirit.

When I become more aware of my relationship with God, when I sit in stillness within His love, I am drawn into a deeper level of passive contemplative prayer, and let go of control of all feeling, and thinking. I feel the Presence of the Holy Spirit before and after the deep experience. Afterwards this wonderful feeling of contentment and happiness comes over me. I feel as if I was awakening within my lover's arms.

Sometimes the Presence comes on me in a rush and I have to stop and think whether what I am feeling is a hot flash. Although they are somewhat similar feelings, they are not the same.

With these feelings, the Gift of Knowledge of what I am feeling either comes with it, or slowly later when I reflect that every time I felt this I was in a certain situation. This is part of discernment.

A "message" in my thinking by this voice I talk

about is almost always preceded or followed by my feeling this Presence of the Holy Spirit. Sometimes I have experienced a bright light around me before I heard the "voice".

A "message" is different than a day-dream or my own thinking, because I can remember it word for word days, even months, later and the thoughts are phrased differently than I would normally phrase them. Often this "message" comes to me out of the blue, out of context to the situation or thoughts that I am presently in. An example of a message I received from God: In order to save money, I decided to skimp on buying firewood. I thought I would just dress warmer during the winter months. It was sometime after I made this decision, while I was mowing the lawn, when the thought came to me very powerfully, that I should be frugal, but not miserly. Not buying firewood was being miserly. God would provide the money, somehow, to pay for it. I believe these thoughts directing me to act in an appropriate manner was God speaking to me.

I bought a few cords of wood, my son showed up one evening with a cord, and the church brought me a cord.

Even a spirit-inspired dream is different than a normal dream in that when I awake I can remember everything within the dream, whereas usually, I forget it the moment I awaken. My spiritual dreams also have some thing to do with God and my relationship with Him.

I have also had this feeling of the Presence of the Holy Spirit come over me for protection. I will be in a friendly conversation, and the Presence will come over me and suddenly this person starts talking inappropriately to me. I have already turned to prayer, so his words bounce off. I have come to realize that this has helped me be centered upon God, and to keep the calm that is within me.

Some people get goosebumps when they feel the Presence of the Holy Spirit yet they are not cold. One person told me she feels the Presence of the Holy Spirit by a soft caress on her cheek as if touched lightly by a finger.

At times I have felt "being filled" with the Holy Spirit. I feel this warmth move throughout my insides. I feel it come up within me and can even point to where it is — at my chest, in my throat, up to my eyes, to the top of my head.

I usually associate this feeling with the Presence of Jesus for that is how I first felt Him when He began instructing me on the meaning of the word submission. Once I experienced wave after wave of love that lasted over a half hour.

"The Power of God's Presence" is manifested to me as a pressure, similar to sitting in a small car and having all the doors slammed at once. That pressure in a car lasts but an instant; but this remains and I can move into it. When I first experienced it, as I described in my account at Medjugorje, I was very uncomfortable, but now I step into it willingly as I feel His Love so powerfully. I feel this Power of God's Presence near a tabernacle or during the Exposition of the Blessed Sacrament. It has pushed me back at a 40 degree angle. It has embraced me, encircling me with healing love. I have felt it in "Holy" churches, where many miracles have taken place. I have felt it in my own parish church. It is very strong at most Charismatic Masses in which the church is filled with people who are on fire with love for God.

Why does it make a difference that there are more healings during a Charismatic Mass? When a teacher enters a classroom at the beginning of the school year, she may not feel love. She might feel question marks, hostility, boredom, but often not love. At the end of the year, if she is a good teacher, she enters her classroom and feels love. Charismatics are alive with the love of Jesus in their hearts. They are not afraid to show openly this love. No barriers are holding it back. As this love flows from each person, uniting with the love of their neighbor, uniting with the love of Mary and all the saints, the church becomes filled with this love that one can feel. This uniting of God's love is very powerful. Is it any wonder that more people are affected by a cure or a healing during this time, when they are embraced by Love?

One speaker mentioned a survey that asked people where they usually felt the Presence of God. While listening to music was listed as number one. People also feel it when standing within the beauty or immensity of nature. The third place is within Church. So when you have beauty and church and music and this union of Love, it is truly awesome.

I began to <u>expect</u> to feel this Power at Charismatic masses. I ended up feeling nothing. When the priest prayed over me, I <u>expected</u> the Holy Spirit to give me a monstrous hug. Nothing. But a few days later, while praying in my bedroom, the Holy Spirit came over me so strongly that I Rested in the Spirit there, alone. The next day I attended Mass in my own little church. As I walked through the doors I felt the Power of God's

PRESENCE OF GOD

Presence I had expected to feel at the Charismatic Mass.

God was teaching me that He is everywhere: in my home, every church, in us and around us. He is there whether He gives us the Gift of feeling His Presence or not. God works through our pastors just as He does through a priest with the Gift of Healing. He exhibits His Presence in more powerful ways in certain places, and His healing powers in more powerful ways through persons He has chosen to be His partners for healing. They have the Gift of stirring into flame the Holy Spirit that is given to us through Baptism and Confirmation. The Holy Spirit heals us spiritually, physically, mentally. All we have to do is turn to Him in faith and love and ask Him.

God is everywhere, in us, and around us. But His Real Presence is in the Eucharist. It is not either/or but rather, both/and. Our greatest Gift we can give to God is Jesus in the Eucharist. It is His greatest gift to us.

Our parish is very small. The church seats 120 people. The Easter following my Baptism of the Spirit, I went to a Holy Thursday service. After this service, Father placed the host, Jesus, in the Monstrance for adoration, for the one hour in remembrance when Jesus asked his disciples, "Can't you spend but one hour with me?"

Father placed the Monstrance on a table placed four feet from the first pew. Then everyone left the church! My friend and myself were the only ones who stayed. We went to the first pew to kneel before Jesus. We couldn't! We could not kneel! A powerful force shoved us away. I went to a pew a few rows back, and there knelt and prayed about this phenomenon. This power, this force, was certainly not coming from a mere piece of bread. Nor was it coming from a piece of gold that the monstrance was made out of. This force could only be from God. The Real Presence of Jesus was before me. I realized I was not worthy to be that close. I was filled with pride, that my friend and I were the only ones smart and humble enough to stay for this hour. Look at us, Lord, aren't we great? All I could do was bow my head and say I was sorry.

In the chapter "Silence that Paralyzes" I relate how I felt that same power when I went close to the tabernacle, only this time, I stepped into it, and it engulfed me, held me, and healed me of a tremendous hurt that I had.

Eternal Father,
open my heart and my eyes to the awareness
of Your Presence in my life and in the Eucharist!

FEAR NOT THE EVIL ONE
For I, the Lord God, will protect you.

I was taught all my life that God is everywhere, in us and around us, yet I still had this concept of a Michelangelo - God who sat up in Heaven. We prayed to Him for BIG things, like world peace and conversion of Russia and to stop droughts or floods. To think that He would care about little ol' me and what I thought or did - nah!

Then came that unforgettable day in church when He hugged me and I felt His love for me. For the first time I realized God cared for me. He made His Presence known to me. This revelation marked a new beginning of our relationship. So many things come to my mind as I write these two paragraphs. So many lessons learned: knowing the Trinity, how Jesus came into my life, books read, the devil, my relationship, visions, etc..

Once I became awakened to the Presence of God in my life, I also became more aware of the presence of the devil. In fact, the devil and what he did to scare me away from God was more real to me at first than the manifestations of the Presence of God.

When we don't care about God or our souls, the devil pretty much leaves us alone. But when we turn toward God, the devil realizes we are serious, and he jumps in vigorously to stop us. Jesus is a gentleman. He stays in the background of our lives until we invite Him in. The devil has no such manners. Remember what we were taught as children? To say, "In the name of Jesus, be gone, Satan. Protect me, Jesus." or else, "In the name of Jesus, get behind me, Satan. Come Holy Spirit, give me strength." These prayers still work.

I have been told to ignore Satan. However, if you don't know how he works, he can get the best of you. St. Teresa of Avila wrote page after page to her sisters at the convent on how the devil worked. It wasn't to frighten them. It was to educate them so they did not fall into his traps.

One extreme is to completely refuse to recognize the devil and say that he does not exist. The other extreme is to see him everywhere, in everyone, and avoid contact with people and kick people out of prayer groups for fear he will spread from them to you.

We pray for the success of our parish retreat or parish mission. We thank Jesus for all the people who are touched by the Holy Spirit. Yet we cannot stop praying for these people the moment the mission is over. Then the temptations begin in earnest. When we recognize someone going through a period of trial, keep them drenched in prayer. We do not have to know the particulars of their problem. God knows what they need.

When we are in the store and are tempted to steal something off the shelf, it is easy to recognize the devil and say, "In the name of Jesus, begone, Satan." But do we recognize him in thinking: "That was a nice experience. It must have been the wonderful music making me think it was God I felt," dismissing the experience since music was involved. Or how about, "That was too scary for me. I don't want anything more to do with those crazy Charismatics." Or perhaps, "Wow, I was Baptized in the Holy Spirit and now have the Gift of

Prophecy; but so and so doesn't. She isn't on the same level as I am."

Another example: "My pastor just doesn't understand! He hasn't been Baptized by the Holy Spirit yet. He doesn't understand the Love that we feel in our prayer groups. He won't let us do what we want. We will let him know our disapproval by not going to his Masses. We will stay home and pray for him instead."

Is there no devil behind all this? Think again.

Remember always: God is for unity. He is not secretive. He is inclusive, not exclusive. He died on the cross for our sins, not for our talents and virtues.

I was awakened at 11:00 one night by a bright light and by extreme heat as it filled my body. I was awake but I had my eyes closed. I became involved in a tremendous battle! I felt light coming into me 20,000 times but leaving me 70,000 times stronger. (These numbers came into my mind during this experience.) I became a weapon. This light, energy, shot out my hand like a laser streak. It zipped and vibrated all around the room. I felt that I was protecting someone from an extremely angry Satan. I never felt in danger myself. I was not afraid, for I knew I was on the winning side.

Then the thought came into my mind to call for reinforcements. It was in the middle of the night! I had been told by a new friend, in case of need, call at any time. I called and said, "I am going through a tremendous battle, please pray for me... Here it comes again."

I was awake! I was not dreaming! I was not hallucinating. I was awake, sitting up in bed, setting the phone down, shooting energy from the Holy Spirit out from my hands at some unseen enemy. I felt that I was fighting for someone's soul. I felt Michael the Archangel fighting at my side.

We won! "Take that! That will teach you to try anything with us!" I felt great. I felt victorious. The joy and the heat stayed with me for some time afterwards.

At 2:30 I was again awakened. I joined 6000 voices lifted in praise to God. (This number is the number that came into my mind. I do not know if it has any significance.) I was so tired I could hardly sing with them, nor hold my hand up, but I was honored to be included with them.

I entered a whole other realm of realty. I could not believe that this was happening. I never in my life imagined such a thing. I am a historian, not a fiction writer. If this was all a dream, I never had such dreams before. Besides, I was awake when this all took place! I had made a phone call in the middle of it.

The same thing happened the next night.

I prayed, "Dear God. What was that battle all about? Who was I protecting?"

The thoughts that entered my mind were, "The battle was for yourself. Satan wanted you. He wasn't expecting such resistance nor such joy in such resistance. Your joy in fighting him was what won the battle. You had no fear. It took Satan by surprise. Few women like to fight. You were a Joan of Arc. Satan also didn't expect you to be so obedient to call your friend for reinforcements. You were losing your strength for it hasn't been built up yet and he could have done damage, if you had not had the surge of energy from your friend's prayers."

I answered, "I wasn't afraid, Lord, for I knew with You on my side, I'd win. I won because You have given me your Holy Spirit. The power of the Holy Spirit shot out of my hands. Thank you, Dear God. May my hands be your instruments."

Was this for real or was it an allegory of how God works? It taught me valuable lessons: One, the devil is real. Two, we defeat the devil only in the power of the Holy Spirit within us. It enters us with much strength, but leaves us, as God's partners, even more powerful. Three, don't be afraid to ask others to keep you covered in prayer. We need intercessory prayer. Four, we need also to pray for others.

Is it any wonder that priests to whom I told this story quizzed me? Was I on any medication? Do I take drugs? Alcohol? Have I been near a hypnotist? No, to all these questions. Only a priest with the gift of healing understood.

It is right to question and sort it all out in your mind to help your faith grow. Local priests sometimes get bombarded with such stories of supernatural phenomena in their parishioners' lives. At first it takes them aback, but after awhile they learn what to expect.

Others have told me similar experiences of the devil attempting to scare them away: they saw the devil's manifestation with their eyes. The saints and the Desert Fathers describe seeing devils. This is a time for strengthening faith; going through the worst alone with no one believing you; turning to and depending totally upon God. I do not write this to frighten people, but, if you should experience such phenomena, know that you are not alone, it will pass, and the devil is powerless against you. God has promised to protect those who turn to and rely on Him.

Song of Hope

You may be labeled a loony when you start describing the things <u>God</u> is doing in your life.

Months passed. I was feeling great. No pain! Then slowly the pain returned. First the stomach aches. Then the back pain and the muscle aches. Well, it was nice while it lasted. But this time the pain was weird. The pain in my muscles was not in muscles that normally hurt. Muscles hurt that I did not use. I really became alarmed when my smile left, and a great depression came over me. What was happening?

I called a priest who was in the Healing Ministry and explained what was happening. He began praying and within minutes all pain was gone! "You were under attack," he told me as he understood.

Now whenever I get pain of any kind, I offer it up to the greater honor and glory of God and I give it to His Son, Jesus, to add to His love. Pain is not from God. It is from natural sources, or else it is from the devil. If I whack my thumb with a hammer, it is going to hurt. That's a natural source of pain. By giving my pain to God, I feel better in my suffering. He may or may not take it away. Grace can be given me, in spite of it. But if the pain is from the devil, it does not last. He does not want it going to the Glory of God. In any case, I win, he loses.

One night I was awakened by a very nasty voice saying, "Watch what I can do." This was an audible voice, one that I heard with my ears. Immediately all the dogs in my neighborhood started barking at once, as if all smelled a bear at the same time. This barking went on and on. I could not go back to sleep. Finally after about twenty minutes I said, "Satan be gone. Lord, come and fill this neighborhood with your Presence. Please quiet these dogs." And immediately came silence!

For the next two nights, the same thing happened. A simple prayer and all the dogs shut up at once. Coincidence? I learned to pray immediately and not wait twenty minutes!

Then, while in church, during the sermon, all the babies started crying at once, as if they had all been pricked with a pin at the same time. I again prayed, "Satan be gone. This is a holy place. Lord, send your angels to sooth these babies." Immediately came silence. As time went on, I learned that the babies often began crying during a crucial part of the sermon. I have guessed that this part was important for someone to hear.

During times of prayer, mosquitoes and biting gnats have suddenly appeared, distracting me. Again, I found that short little prayer to be mighty powerful. They're gone in an instant.

Distractions during prayer are permitted by God. He allows this test for you to turn to Him in a different way, to see His power in a different light. Don't get mad or discouraged or become prideful over your time alone with God. Then you lose the grace you would have gained.

After a Healing Mass, you may feel much in peace. You want to sit and bask in this feeling of love. So what happens? Your husband insists on watching wrestling. Your sons make fun of your spaced out attitude. Your daughters have their rock music turned up full blast. Your friend calls to complain that the pastor got mad at something the Healing priest said during the service and said he won't have him back. A prayer group leader blew up and called someone names and made her cry. Who's behind all this? Coincidence you say? There is no such thing as a devil, you say? Be aware of him trying to destroy your peace, your marriage, your friendships, your prayer groups.

God has given me the Gift of Discernment, in one case it is the supersensitivity to these spirits. The first time I noticed this was when I came upon my son and his friend playing "Dungeons and Dragons." I had heard this was a bad game, but I thought that was only if you believed it was bad. If you didn't believe it, it just wasn't so. No harm could come of it. As I came near the table, I felt something moving away from me - scattering in fear from me. I felt this movement and I felt this fear. I was given the knowledge that what I sensed were evil spirits.

After that incident I could often feel evil spirits as they entered the house with the teenagers. I sensed these spirits as they spread about the house as smoke would. Suddenly they encountered me. "Be gone!" sent them flying.

One time I was at the computer. I had praise music on. The teenagers came in. They left my music on. "Sam" paced about the house and every time he came near me, I felt this negativity around him. I felt as if evil spirits were clinging to him instead of flowing all about the house as they usually did. Then "Sam" began talking to me. "Mom and I just had a fight."

I said a silent prayer. He talked some more. Soon he said, "This music sure is peaceful." Then, "Your house sure is peaceful. I like it here."

What is the lesson here? That I should not have teenagers in my house? I'm letting evil spirits in with them? No. The boy was upset over a fight with his mom. He was hurt. The devil wanted to poke at and strengthen this hurt and turn it into division between his mother and himself. Perhaps even into a hatred. We should keep our friends covered in prayer, especially teenagers. And we should pray for peace in our homes that our children have a peaceful place to come to.

After some time I began to think what a wonderful warrior I was for God. All I had to do was say, "Boo" and I scared the evil spirits away. Me afraid? Of what?

No, we should not be afraid, but we should recognize who is really protecting us. It is not me, Kathy Moore, whom the devil fears but Jesus within me and beside me.

This was brought home to me one day. I imagined myself as a little girl hanging onto Jesus' hand with my right hand. In my left hand I had a toy wooden sword. I poked and slashed with this sword and fought imaginary boogie men.

This little day dream suddenly became so real that I actually began to act it out in my living room.

I pictured myself, now grown up. I no longer needed to hang onto the hand of Jesus. I was now going to be His warrior. I was going to fight along side St. Michael the Archangel and all the saints who were exorcists. I was now old enough and powerful enough to go it alone. So I let go of Jesus' hand.

The little tiny boogie man in front of me suddenly enlarged himself to fill the whole room. He became a terrifying monster. I shrunk back down to little girl size, ran and hid behind Jesus and clung to his robe. He laughed and with one swift kick sent that monster howling as it evaporated into the air.

The lesson I learned that day was that we indeed must be as little children and never let go of Jesus' hand. It is Jesus who protects us. Through His power we are saved. How many times have we heard this? This little make-believe incident was very real to me. It was more real than practicing an act in my drama class. This little make-believe incident truly humbled me. No one can convince me this was all part of my imagination and none of it from God. The lesson sunk in deep.

I was shown another form of a very powerful evil spirit. I stopped at a stranger's house to ask an elderly lady for help on a community project. A very pleasant conversation was going when suddenly her attitude changed. She began complaining about the vandalism of kids, about the strangers appearing in our town, about these weird men with long flowing hair our children were imitating. Her prejudices, her fears, her hates spewed out of her mouth. As she talked, a great tiredness came over me. I couldn't argue back. This lady suddenly turned against me, against my project, and refused her help. She asked me to leave.

The next night I was talking with some very Christian men. The topic turned to helping the poor through the St. Vincent de Paul organization. Suddenly the tone of the men's voices changed to sarcastic descriptions of these poor who were out to take advantage of the system, who couldn't budget their $800 a month welfare money so they had to return each month for a hand-out. The prejudice against the poor came out. As they talked, again, a great tiredness came over me. I no longer wanted to be part of this conversation and left.

FEAR NOT THE EVIL ONE

I began to realize that I had encountered a more powerful evil spirit than one I had gotten rid of in my home. This one didn't flee when I was near. This one didn't scatter when I said, "Boo." It was preying on the hatreds and the prejudices within the people. I had been tempted to join in this negative conversation, to be roped in, drawn in to this negative way of thinking. God had let me feel this evil spirit in the form of my tiredness. By myself, I was defenseless.

The lesson here is that destructive talk is instigated by the devil. Don't be roped into it. He has no power over you. Pray instead for the people who are negative, for the healing of their hurts, and the resulting prejudices to be healed. I have no idea if my prayers for these people have taken effect, but I do know by saying a prayer silently during the conversation I stopped feeling the tiredness and I was also able to withstand the temptation of joining in the negative conversation.

The third form of evil spirit I have encountered I call a cold spirit. It comes creeping over me during prayer time. It took awhile but I have learned that it is a distracting spirit. I prayed so long and hard against it, I failed to hear the talk given. I noticed that it came from a certain direction, I prayed, and I no longer felt it after the person next to me got up and gave their testimony. I wondered if perhaps it was trying to discourage her from doing so.

I learned to pray, "I offer this cold spirit up to You, Oh God, all for Your greater honor and glory! Please fill me with the warmth of Your Holy Spirit, and every time I feel this cold spirit may a thousand souls be released into heaven." It always instantly leaves me. If it should come back during the prayer session, rather than say the long prayer, I simply say, "There goes a thousand souls." And it is gone.

I have never, personally met an evil person. I have felt evil within a room. I have heard of evil people spitting on crucifixes, torturing people. I won't say they don't exist. I believe their hurts grew into such a fear and hate that they shut out completely all love within them. They have never experienced human love. They have never been taught about God or hope or that God's love even exists.

My eternal Father, I fear no evil for You are with me.

THANK YOU FOR THIS HEALING

My aunt was diagnosed with a very rare brain tumor. Our family and friends prayed for her. A specialist performed the operation and deemed it a success, from a medical view point. My aunt Ginny could not return home. She had to remain the rest of her days living at a nursing home within minutes of the hospital. She showed no interest in life.

My uncle could no longer afford the care facility. Prayer requests for my aunt were again sent out. My uncle then reported that the new care facility, although lacking material amenities, had a staff filled with love.

I saw my uncle at our family reunion. He was telling everyone the words my aunt spoke right before he left. "Aren't you going to comb my hair? I can't go out in the hallway like this... Where's my dress? I can't go out in the hallway wearing this gown... I need make-up on. Where's my lipstick?"

And then came the clincher, the statement that filled everyone with hope. "When are you going to take me shopping?"

Within a few months my uncle took my aunt home and reported that she is her old self again. In fact she looks years younger. "This is truly an answer to prayers."

We give praise and thanksgiving to You, O Lord.

My mom's cousin's son had epilepsy. It got so

bad that his seizures became continuous and it was only a matter of time before he would die.

His father, Jim, could no longer stand waiting in his son's hospital room and so went out to walk the halls. He met a man in the hallway who greeted Jim by name and seemed to know all about his son's condition. Jim figured that this man worked in the hospital. Jim was asked by the man if he would like to pray with him in the chapel and so they went in together. Jim was not a religious man and so would not have gone into that room by himself. When he came out he noticed a lot of activity around his son's room. He thought, "I only left for a few minutes and now my son has died."

His son's seizures had stopped. Not only that but no scar tissue remained on his brain indicating that he ever had a seizure! The fact that he was an epileptic was erased from his medical record and he later had a career in the military.

When Jim described the man he had met in the hallway to the hospital personnel, no one knew him. He realized this man was an angel from God and he became very active within the Baptist Church.

We give praise and thanksgiving to You, O Lord.

My cousin Mike told me that twelve years ago he and his wife joined a nondenominational prayer group. There were twelve people in it. Today that prayer group is one thousand strong. He said that both he and his wife experienced a healing from the addictions of smoking and alcohol.

We give praise and thanksgiving to You, O Lord.

My auntie Kay told me that she had to have an operation on her temple. The doctor said that she would have a terrible headache when she came out from under the anesthesia. Waiting for the operation, she was in excruciating pain from an incision from a heart operation she had the year before. She prayed for relief from this pain, but said she didn't mention the soon-to-be headache. Low and behold, all pain left her. Her incision stopped hurting and she never had the predicted headache. "God not only took away the pain that I asked Him to, He threw in the bonus of no headache as well." She never again experienced pain from either operation.

We give praise and thanksgiving to You, O Lord.

A mother told me that her daughter was terribly addicted to drugs. She shot cocaine into her arms and when they hurt too much, she took morphine. This mother prayed to the Blessed Virgin Mary to help her daughter help herself get off drugs. That was in 1980 and two weeks after the prayer the daughter went into the drug rehabilitation program by her own will and has been off drugs ever since. She is now a successful business woman. God healed the daughter because of the mother's prayers. Even though the daughter still does not pray nor recognize any divine help in her recovery.

We give praise and thanksgiving to You, O Lord.

A grandmother told me of the loss of her granddaughter, whom she thought of as her own daughter. The little girl was killed by a drunk driver at the age of three and this woman could not get over her death. I talked to the grandfather, a Lutheran, who has a terminal illness. The doctors had given "Ed" a few months to live — that was four years before. "Ed" told me that a few months ago, he had gotten very sick, and thought that this time he was surely going to die. His little granddaughter suddenly appeared to him in his room. She was there. He saw her. He wasn't on medication. He saw her. He asked, "Does this mean I will join you soon?"

"No, Grandpa. Your time isn't ready yet."

God had given him the Gift of knowing his granddaughter was in Heaven. "Ed" said he had never told this story to anyone before. Who would believe him?

We give praise and thanksgiving to You, O Lord.

An elderly friend of mine was at a retreat. As she stood by a statue of our Lady of Sorrows she smelled roses. There weren't any flowers growing near by. Then she heard her father's voice audibly in her ear, "Marie, I am so proud of the path you have chosen." Her father had died many years before. Again, God had given Marie the Gift of knowing he was in Heaven. He also let her know in this way that He was pleased with her life.

We give praise and thanksgiving to You, O Lord.

During a Healing Mass a couple (friends of mine) went up as intercessors for their relative living in another city. The relative had an operation. Afterwards she had to have a urine bag. Within days after the Healing Mass this relative was completely healed.

We give praise and thanksgiving to You, O Lord.

A friend, Gail, related this story to me: Gail's brother-in-law was traveling to join his wife. Although it was late at night, and he was not a good night driver, he was anxious to be with her and so continued on his journey. His route took him through a river canyon. The road twists with a steep cliff on one side and a sheer drop into the canyon on the other.

Gail awoke at midnight and thought of her brother-in-law. She immediately began praying for him. She learned later that her sister also awoke at midnight and began praying.

Early in the morning, a lady was walking her dog along the canyon road and she discovered a car way down over the embankment. She hurried home and called 911. The highway patrol found the brother-in-law hanging upside down by his seat belt within the car. When they called Gail's sister, they didn't offer much hope. They figured he had hung upside down for at least six hours. They thought the accident occurred around midnight. His head was grossly swollen. If he did live, there would be extensive brain damage.

Gail and her sister called their prayer chains and waited in hope. Slowly, miraculously the brother-in-law recovered. He is a lawyer and continues to practice law. He won an award in recognition of his service.

Several months after the accident, Gail's sister called the woman who found the car in order to thank her. The woman said, "You know, I would have never spotted the car if it didn't have this light all around it. The car glowed."

We give praise and thanksgiving to You, O Lord.

God is manifesting His Presence to thousands of people all over the world, right now. During our life-time. Come! Believe! Hope! Love!

Father, I thank you for doing the most needful, loving thing in my life right now.

COME TO MY HOUSE

I was praying one Saturday afternoon and then I became as still as possible to listen. Inside me I heard a faint voice say, "Come to My house."

Was it the voice of Jesus within me? I didn't know, but it wouldn't hurt to go. It was 4:00. Since my teenage son had the car I had to walk to church two miles away. I figured I'd be home by 6.

At the church I prayed for awhile and then became aware that the flowers by the altar were all dead. Not just dried up but keeled over. Dead. It was Saturday night. Whoever was supposed to clean the church for Sunday was getting a late start. I could help by changing the flowers. Our church has a Mary's Garden and one yellow rose bush had enough blossoms to fill all the vases I needed.

Then I noticed the Holy Water Founts needed filling. After that was done I noticed that the pews needed dusting. Our pastor had been sandblasting the windows and so the pews were coated with a thick layer of dust. I found a rag and furniture polish and dusted the pews. If I didn't sweep between the pews and the windows people would crunch, crunch, crunch when they walked there. So I swept — and vacuumed. It was 9:00 by the time I got home.

I did not see all that needed to be done at once. I

saw only one thing at a time. Each in itself was easy to do. Looking at the whole might have been too over-whelming for me. Am I to clean this whole church by myself?

I called my pastor that night because the votive light by the tabernacle was almost out and he would have to bring some more candles when he came. I also told him how I had come to the church after hearing this quiet voice inside me.

I was in awe that God had asked me to come to clean His house. It had a different effect on me than if someone had phoned and asked me to clean the church. Father was very grateful that I had done so. We were having a visiting priest come for Mass the next day and Father said he would have been very embarrassed if the church had been in the condition that I had found it. I thought later that the whole congregation would have been embarrassed.

I later learned that the person assigned to clean the church that month had just been diagnosed with cancer. She surely had too many other things on her mind than to remember that her name was posted in the back of the church.

I am shown a lesson from God, but I keep learning new things from this lesson. God opens my eyes. He opens my eyes through a sermon, through scripture, through a passage in a book, through a friend. As He revealed the chores needing to be done in the church one by one, so He reveals Himself to me, a little here, a little there.

Sometimes I think I am so dumb. I was telling a friend, Carey, about this incident, still in awe that God had asked me to come and clean His house.

Carey said, "Not only would your pastor and your congregation be embarrassed, but Jesus would have been embarrassed. He is the host. He invites us all to His house on Sunday. As any host, He wants a clean house. But He has no hands. but ours."

"HAS NO HANDS!" Bells rang in my head! God has given me devotion to the Infant Jesus of Prague, and I have read hundreds of times the message that came from the statue of the Infant Jesus for Fr. Cyril, "Have mercy on Me and I will have mercy on you. GIVE ME HANDS and I will give you Peace. The more you honor Me, the more I will bless you."

I have before me, right by my computer the words of St. Teresa of Avila: "Christ has no body now on earth but yours, no hands but yours, no feet but yours. Yours are the eyes with which Christ must express compassion towards the world. Yours are the feet with which Christ is to go about doing good. Yours are the hands with which Christ is to bless humanity now."

How many times have I read this? Yet, for the first time I SAW what it meant. My eyes were opened to its meaning.

I was in awe of this lesson as I sat in the church and realized God had called me to clean His House. I was in awe again when I talked to Father and the lesson took on a deeper meaning. God would show me what He wants in steps. And then when I talked with my friend the lesson went still deeper, "we are His hands," bringing again a sense of awe.

Carey, who has the Gift of Prophecy, with tears running down her cheek, gave me a prophetic word.

"Kathy, you are to clean the church." She added, "I don't mean physically."

How God reveals himself to us are our personal experiences with God. We cannot prove they are from God. I cannot prove that the voice quietly whispered in my mind, "Come to my house", was from God and not from my imagination. But God drew me to Himself through this experience. He revealed Himself to me in ways I needed and in ways in which I learn.

The experience is important, yes. But the experience may happen only once. The lesson learned should live on and ring true and draw us closer to God of all truth. The lesson learned should be in accordance with Scripture and the teachings of the Catholic Church. The Catholic Church has 2000 years of recorded personal experiences with God. The writings of the Saints are available for all to read.

Open your mind to seeing God's Presence in your life. See that the church is His House and He invites us to spend time with Him often. Go there with respect and adoration. Open your heart to the responsibility of being His hands, His feet, His voice to the world.

God has not made His Presence known to me so only I can enjoy Him. I am to give witness. I encourage you to believe, to turn to Him. He is available to everyone. His love and forgiveness is for everyone. Just ask!

Jesus, my Lord, open my eyes
to Your Presence in my life.

SO YOU AREN'T BELIEVED!

One day I overheard my teenage son talking on the telephone. I don't normally eavesdrop. I don't normally hear him talking when he's on the phone. This day I was even taking a nap. I awoke and heard him say:

"It's scary at first. You're standing right on the edge. It really takes courage to take the first step. But once you do there's no turning back. It's awesome. Simply awesome."

I went back to sleep and a little while later, awoke and heard him say this:

"It becomes your whole life. It's all you want to think about. Talk about. And you want everyone to try it."

When he hung up I went downstairs and said, "You know. What you were saying. That's how I feel about God."

He answered, "But Mom. I was talking about snowboarding. That's just one tiny phase of a person's life. God is ...". He moved his hands in big circles to indicate "everything."

My son is proud to say he's a snowboarding fanatic. So, if I'm called a religious fanatic, that's OK.

I was talking to a close friend whom I had not seen for some time. She complained about an acquaintance who always wanted to talk about her own agenda and, when she was done, had nothing more to say. Are we not all like that? We talk about what interests and concerns us?

I've met the most famous man in the world and he's fallen in love with me and I with him. With me, of all people! A king, falling in love with me! I want to tell the whole world! That's all I want to talk about, my life with him, the gifts he's given me! I want to shout it from the roof tops! The difference is, with a human king, I would be jealous if other people fell in love with him. With my king, I want the whole world to come to know and experience His love.

Our journey to God is often alone. Our friends, our family may not want to hear talk about religion. We may not be believed. If they do believe us, they may not understand.

When I started having intense and enlightening experiences from God I met with skepticism. It seems everyone does. Even Jesus' relatives wanted to pull him away from his preaching and take him home. Some said He was possessed by an evil spirit.

Some people have had religious experiences and not been helped by their priests or ministers. Do not give up nor turn away from the Church because some of your co-religionists do not understand and believe you. This can be the hardest time in your life, especially if, besides not being believed, you are called evil.

St. Teresa of Avila went through such trials. She had a difficult time finding a spiritual director who believed her. When her best friends called her evil, she felt this experience was the worst. If you survive with your mind in tact, according to Teresa, be thankful, for other trials are less in comparison. She said to give your reputation to God. You are in His hands.

God-experience is ineffable. You know it is from God, but you don't know. I mean, this is God! Communicating with me! And who am I? No one. Why would He do such a thing for me? You want help in sorting it all out. You want confirmation. You want affirmation. And you do not receive it from others. This seems to be something many of us go through. Alone.

God will never leave us alone. We may think we are, but we are not. Faith is truly tested at this time. God is responsible for this experience, this unique moment of grace. You have to cling to this moment for you will be buffeted on all sides. Prayer and daily Mass, and Communion will nourish and give you more strength.

If this is truly an experience of God, you will feel the awesomeness of it and the littleness of yourself. You will want to do anything and everything that He asks of you. A good spiritual director can help you recognize and discern the fruits of the Holy Spirit — wisdom, piety, counsel, fear of the Lord, understanding, knowledge, fortitude, growing within.

A very important and basic gift of the Holy Spirit is forgiveness. This is one thing a competent spiritual director will look for within you. All the gifts and powerful manifestations of God are of little avail if we do not forgive. We need to forgive everyone else for not believing us, for perhaps insulting us. We need to celebrate Mass each Sunday and, if possible, daily Mass, not because this is a requirement of the Catholic Church, but because this is what God wants and invites us there.

Be humble enough to go to your own pastor for

confession. This may be extremely hard, when you are trying to convince him that you have had a religious experience. Your priest has to see an honest struggle within you. Experiencing God may not change us overnight, but we ought to cooperate with God's direction. A person does not become a Saint and then experience God. God manifests Himself to sinners, who then struggle to become better. We hold up the Saints as examples and reassurance that this struggle is worth the effort. The fight to overcome our weaknesses and our faults can be won.

If people do not understand, do not condemn them. They were not given this gift at this time. It has nothing to do with ignorance nor is it an indication of their spiritual level.

Pray before entering a Christian bookstore, so that you will be led to the book God prefers for you, one that will affirm your experiences. Pray before opening the Bible, so that the Word of God can speak more effectively to you. Pray for the gifts of understanding and discernment, and genuine love and compassion for all who do not understand you.

Lord, Jesus Christ,
help me through the times when I am not believed,
am mocked and scorned. Help me to forgive those
responsible. Help me become anchored in you and not
wallow in the hurt, the anger and bitterness I feel.

HE IS WITH US ALWAYS

Prayer is communicating with God: nurturing a personal relationship, getting to know Him better. Some say they are too busy. They don't have the time or can't be bothered. Some give thanks for their meals, for the day. Some pray when they need help to pass a test, to get the hay in before it rains, etc.. We worship the Lord. We give Him praise, for He is with us always.

When we are hurt, God cares. He consoles us with friends, teaches us, guides us, if we let Him, for He is with us always.

Recite memorized prayers. Read the Sacred Scriptures. Honor Mary and fight evil by praying the rosary. It is powerful. Meditate. Think about what you are saying, what you are reading, what you are singing. Mean what you say. Say what you mean. Be aware of God at all times, for He is with us always.

Sing songs of praise and worship. The sacrifice of praise is pleasing to the Lord. Sing His praises all day long, for He is with us always.

Speak with Him. Ask Him for what you need and want. Give Him thanks, and listen. Be still. Be patient. We will not hear Him properly unless we are attentive. It takes time. Give yourself totally to the Lord. God communicates with you. Listen, for He is with us always.

He speaks to us in our thoughts. He brings solutions to problems. He explains behavior, points out wrongs, reinforces good, clarifies truth, reminds us of the needy — the lonely, sick, elderly, those who need prayers, and healing. He awakens us in the night. Pray. He wants us to. He wants our cooperation, for He is with us always.

Ask the Holy Spirit to fill you and surround you. Ask to be changed, healed physically, mentally, spiritually. Ask for forgiveness, and for the Gift of forgiving others. Invite God to work in your life. Consecrate yourself to Him, to His heart, to His mother's heart, for He is with us always.

Pray for all others, for our families, for healing of memories, for all of God's gifts. Pray to grow more deeply into Him. Pray especially for Faith, Hope and Love. Give thanks to the Lord, for He is good. Give Him praise. He hears us, for He is with us always.

Be aware of being His hands, helping others. Be aware that you are His voice. Invite Him to speak through you. You are His compassion, feel it. You are His love, show it, for He is with us always.

Some He will draw into deeper silence. Thoughts become more of Him: "We praise You. We love You. Have mercy on us. Forgive us." God is love, for He is with us always.

He takes us into His heart. He engulfs us in a cocoon of love. When we emerge, we know not what fully happened to us, but that we are changed. Give Him an hour of praise even in silence. Give Him an hour before the Blessed Sacrament. Come to adore Him, for He is with us always.

Go to sleep each night with words of praise and thanksgiving flowing through your mind. Awake each morning proclaiming praise and thanksgiving to the Lord, for He is with us always.

Talk to him, continue to know Him better, for He is with us always.

BE PRESENT TO GOD

If we experience God's Presence, it is very easy to say it was a coincidence. No mere coincidence can produce genuine God-experience. If we become certain that God indeed soaks and saturates us with His presence, then we want to change, to be more God-oriented.

Once I did not truly believe that the bread and wine turned into the body and blood of Jesus. I prayed for help to eliminate my unbelief. I was awakened in the night with a box of light around me. I thought, "Lord, I do not know what this means. You are the potter. I am the clay. Mold me. Meld me." and I went back to sleep.

In the morning I realized I was a changed person.

One day I didn't believe and the next day I was certain that it was true. How can I describe the difference? How can I describe the change?

I was changed and I wanted to respond to God. I truly believed this experience was from God. Going to church was no longer a matter of Sunday obligation. Going to daily Mass became a treasured grace. I believed everything I had been taught about the Eucharist. I could no longer day dream through the Mass. What was going on at the altar became very important. My presence, my total awareness, was now necessary. My Lord was right there! He was my food, my strength, my nourishment, the healing power within me. He was the source of all Grace I would need until I was able to receive Him again.

It reminds me, in a way, of these computer games we play. I love them and have played a good many of them. As we fight the bad guys and, in turn, we are injured, our strength gets less and less. We have to find the energy pellets and eat them to get our strength back. I hate to compare receiving Our Lord in Communion with a video game, but the further from Mass we get, the weaker we become to resisting temptations. We need the Eucharist to become strong again. We need the Eucharist daily.

If I truly believe God called me to church and revealed to me one thing at a time which needed cleaning, I was urged to change. I asked, "What is God teaching me now?" He taught me that He would show me step by step what He would like me to do for Him. What He would ask of me would not be such that I would turn back in despair. Then He gave me genuine awe when my friend said, "Jesus is the host. He wants a clean house. But He has no hands."

This awe, I knew, was my eyes, my inner awareness, being opened. God wanted to teach me that we are His hands, His feet, His voice, His compassion, His love. His light within us is example to the world. Do we show it? Do we freely maintain His church, teach CCD, feed the poor, trust Him to show us, step by step, the things we have to do?

I should change if I truly believe that it was God teaching me.

I suffered many hurts in life and became bitter and

angry. The least little incident would hurt my feelings, bring me to tears and I would react unkindly. I had to learn to pray for those who hurt me. I still didn't change. The next day was no different. I finally realized that whenever I gave a problem to God, I hung on to it for dear life. God wouldn't play the tug-of-war game with me. He just let go and let me have the problem back.

It was not until I spent a Sunday, alone in my bedroom, and gave the entire day to God, along with all my problems, hurts, sins, talents, everything, that my life started to change. I asked for help in forgiving others. I asked for my barriers to be removed. Gradually things which once hurt me, no longer did. As new hurts surfaced, I learned to keep giving them to God. Indeed they surfaced!

I asked for help in trusting Him. I remember sitting on the couch, knowing I should go to the computer and write, but I was petrified. I could not move. I was afraid of the future, afraid of failing: What if my writing was not good enough to be accepted? I was afraid of succeeding. What would happen if I became successful and my friends stopped associating with me? Everyone said my last article was terrific. How can I possibly write another one as good? I was so afraid of the future, I couldn't move off the couch to begin to write.

I gave my fear to God and He took it. He healed me. Yes, sometimes I am afraid, but not as before. My future is in His hands.

Jesus, Son of the Living God,
send the Holy Spirit to give me the Gifts
I need to be responsive to Your constant Presence.

WRITE

My hand will not move.
It lies still across the page
The pen poised, the fingers curled.
But the mind sends no signal.
A word comes to the surface,
Another, and then another.
All unrelated.

No, I cannot write that.
She will hear and get mad.
Fear.

No, I cannot write that.
That strikes too close to home.

Can I bare my true feelings,
My experiences with life?

What will people say?
What will they think?

Be careful.

But isn't that what I want?
To write what people relate to,
What people understand,
To open their eyes,
To, if possible,

Song of Hope

To change the world —
The way we think.
To point out truth?
Do people still search for truth?
Do I have it?
Is it just my point of view?

Write!

Let others decide
To agree or disagree.
But write.

LOVE ME. SIMPLY LOVE ME.

I continually ask God, "What do You want me to do?"
Does God want something from me?

The only answer I get back from God is, "Love me.
Simply love me."

Wait a minute! What does this mean? Who am I
to love God! This means more than reciting a memorized
prayer, "God, I love You above all things, with my whole
heart and soul, because You are all-good and worthy of
all love." This is more than just loving my neighbor and
forgiving him.

I no longer really loved anyone, let alone God.
Could I give myself in love to anyone ever again? Where
would God take me? What would He ask me to do? What
would He ask me to give up? Could I give up my independence? Did I want to?

This decision seemed similar to deciding to marry
someone. Do we really know what our husband will be
like? Where will we live? What will we be doing? How
will he treat us?

Then I thought of the mail-order brides, who left
homes and traveled to distant lands to meet prospective
husbands, not having any idea what they would be like,
how they would treat them.

I didn't know what God looked like. Did it mat-

97

ter? I can only love in human ways. I am not a God. I am a human. Do looks matter? Stories said that if you looked upon the face of God, you died. Was He so ugly?

I only knew God by the gifts He had showered on me — my sons, my home, my family, the beauty of nature. All that God gives us is good. God is love. Saying "yes" to love God was similar to saying "yes" to a husband and becoming a mail-order bride. I wasn't going to be promised happiness or a grand and glorious place to live. I was promised that He would love me. I just had to trust Him.

To love someone properly demands commitment. Was I ready to give up myself for another? To give up my independence? To put my faith and trust in Him? To put my life in His hands? Someone I could not see? Someone in whom I was just asked to believe?

I said, "Yes. I will love You."

Awesome days followed!

God comes to those whom He has chosen whenever they desire, for He gives them this desire.

I had suffered much the previous year — a headache for nine days, loss of a good friend, deep misunderstandings, and slander against me. But the lessons I learned! Trust in God was formed and barriers to accepting God's love were removed. My happiness the year before was more selfish. God's love for me felt good. I wanted more. But I did not properly return this love. I could not let go of my fears, and totally trust. Finally, with God's help, I was able to let go. I took the giant leap of faith — and soared!

I am in love with God!

I feel the Presence of the Holy Spirit come over

me and it stays. It fans the fire of love in me. What awesome love!

My days are spent alone in silence, and at certain times I withdraw into myself to be with God — away from other thoughts, books, writing, housework. I look forward to these times, as if to spend a few minutes with an intimate lover. The Song of Songs comes to my mind then, for I am seeking my Lover.

The smile on my face, radiating this love, this happiness within me, is the outward appearance!

Joy wells up from deep inside for absolutely no reason whatsoever. Alone and smiling from ear to ear, ready to burst into song, filled with happiness — this is from God.

I am so happy, so much in love — in love with God! It is unbelievable, intangible, indescribable. Yet it is so real. I want everyone to experience this, yet words cannot even get them interested. Once they do, they, too, will want to tell the whole world.

My spiritual director assured me that what I was experiencing was OK. Go with it. She gave me the confirmation I needed. And all stops were pulled out.

I feel ashamed that my director had to point out to me the great Gift of love God has given me. I am not worthy of it. I still ask, "Why me?" I still am tempted to think, "My prayers aren't answered.... I don't have any charismatic gifts."

I feel as if dancing on air, soaring with eagles! Sometimes I think of God and I can feel my soul begin to sing. Sometimes, afterwards, I feel reluctant to function, to think, to do anything, but to forget all.

I cannot describe adequately how I feel, so it is

with great pleasure that I read the writings of the mystics. St. Teresa of Avila and the author of the Cloud of Unknowing, as well as other authors writing about contemplative prayer, describe this experience. As I read them, my soul again sings. Here is someone who understands!

When I read their descriptions of this love, God kindles my love for Him all the more. He gives me knowledge and afterwards I can better explain spiritual experiences. He gives me understanding of scripture. I recognize what is happening to me. Yes! That is how it is! I know! I understand!

The very first time God drew me into passive contemplative prayer, I was sitting at my computer. Suddenly my body became weak, my mind blank save for the word, "Pray". I felt, what I came to know, the Presence of the Holy Spirit coming over me. I knew I was praying, yet my mind was blank. I was not praying with my intellect but with my heart and soul. Because of that word, "Pray", I knew this was from God.

Because the deepest level is so much like sleep, I depend on that feeling of the Holy Spirit coming first. Then when I awaken, I feel as someone satiated in love and lying in their lover's arms, and very, very happy.

During these times I am aware of nothing happening to me, except in rare instances when God enlightens me. For example, the time when the light of the Holy Spirit surrounded me and the following morning I realized that my faith had magnified. One time I "saw" God kissing my soul, His caresses fanning the flame of the fire of love. After that experience I "floated" for several weeks.

My pastor said that I had to find my own way

down to earth. I had to find a balance. He found this balance between earth and heaven by becoming a priest.

I had to have help and, so, I sought a spiritual director. Some were also saying that what I was experiencing was not from God, but that I was possessed by the devil. I sought a director who knew and understood St. Teresa of Avila, and contemplative prayer.

I might go several weeks without feeling my soul do flip flops over the thought of God. I begin to yearn for Him. Then the next week I can barely function as I become absorbed in God.

Sometimes I just step outdoors and God's love becomes so overpowering I cannot move. I stand there like a statue. I am still aware of others and I wonder what the neighbors would think if they saw me standing so still for so long. My absorption in God is far from complete, but God forgives me for my failures.

I pray that everyone in the whole world will experience this love, this experience of God's presence in their lives. Are such prayers answered? Maybe not in ways we expect.

I had a dream. A man was on a bridge. I was behind him and to his left. As he looked, I saw what he saw. He looked up at the sky and the stars. I had never seen so many before. The beauty was awesome!

The man looked out over the water and the waves and ripples reflected star light and moon light. It was beautiful!

The man looked at the horizon and saw the lights of the city. Everywhere in the darkness was beauty.

The man spoke. "Ah, what beauty! I have never seen the night so beautiful. It is magnificent! God, you have shown this beauty to me tonight. I came here to end it all. To jump off this bridge. But this beauty! I know you have shown it to me to let me know you are with me. Thank you, Lord."

A voice behind me and to my left said, "This man was shown such great beauty because of your prayers."

Dear Lord, help me accept Your love for me and give me love for You.

I HAD A DREAM

I had four dreams. In the first, I dreamed I had died. I saw this dead body lying face down on the ground. Her head was toward a marker, like a tombstone or rather an historical marker. The body wasn't in a cemetery; there weren't other markers around. The head was all bloody, and the glass from broken eye glasses led in a trail to her face. People were standing around her, but doing nothing. The body was wearing what I wear now, sweater and pants, and her hair was how I have it now, not grey, or different. As I moved to the side to get a better look, the body raised its head and looked toward me and I saw that it was me. The me in my dream screamed in pain and agony.

I had not remembered any of my dreams over the previous year but this one was remembered in every detail. Because I had been praying for God to reveal His plan for me, I thought this was it. I was going to die a horrible, painful death. It frightened me very much. I did not want to die and yet I thought, if all this happening to me were from God, wouldn't I want to die and be with Him in heaven? I thought my death in the dream to be such a waste. Frankly, I'd prefer to die peacefully in my sleep, not some violent death. And then I thought my life such a waste. What had I done with it? I had to get with it and do something! [My plans for a trip to

Song of Hope

Wisconsin to see relatives, which I will relate in another chapter, sprang from this dream. I felt that if I were to die soon, I wanted to see my family.]

I told a close friend, Carey, about this dream. She has read much about interpreting dreams. She interpreted my dream as religious, full of symbolism. It didn't mean my physical death but spiritual death to self. The blood was from all the injuries that I suffered. The historical marker was perhaps a symbol of the historical movie script I was writing. People doing nothing was a symbol of my dying alone, with no help from others. The broken glasses were a symbol God's path for me as not clearly visible. My scream signified my death to self as very painful.

When I talked with Carey, I tried to express how lonely I was but I could not say the words, "I am lonely," out loud without crying. Carey sensed that something significant was happening to me. She also said that these sorts of dreams sometimes come in threes. Actually I had four dreams. Someone else told me that four symbolizes completeness.

A few days later thoughts of loneliness flooded within me, forcing out other thoughts. I was not only lonely for the moment, but for all the loneliness I've felt during my whole life. All hurts and rejections of my whole life seemed to come to mind. I remembered teachers making fun of me in front of the class; birthday parties when I sat waiting, and no one came. I remembered asking people to join me at a restaurant and no one would come and I didn't want to tell them it was my birthday and make them feel guilty. I remembered cruel remarks of playmates. I remembered calling friends to come to a movie with me and after numerous refusals, I went alone. I remembered not being trusted, being falsely accused, being dismissed from people's houses, not being loved or recognized for who I am.

I cried all day long.

My thoughts were such: "You think you've been lonely in the past. It is nothing compared to the loneliness you will feel if you give yourself to God. For once you do, He will abandon you and you will no longer feel His presence and His love which gives you happiness now. You will truly be lonely then. God wants all your friends. He wants your sons and grandchildren. He's a jealous God and wants you all to Himself."

I finally thought, "OK, if that is what you want, God. I give it all to You."

The realization came to me that in all the times of loneliness, Jesus had been with me. He is compassionately aware of the hurts of everyone.

Once I accepted loneliness and rejection as part of life, once I forgave others for this hurt, the devil no longer had a hold on this pain to blow it out of proportion. God does not will that we be lonely or rejected by others.

Once I gave this pain and hurt to God, accepting it, the devil no longer had a grip upon me in that area. And it was the devil, trying to tempt me away from loving God, who gave me those thoughts that God, too, would reject me once I turned to Him.

I was healed that day.

I can now say, without crying, the words I couldn't say to my friend Carey. "I am lonely." I was rejected and hurt by others, but the pain is now gone. I have felt loneliness since that day, but it has been mild and fleeting.

Song of Hope

Two days after this struggle with loneliness, I had another dream. This time a man was trying to kill me. He hit me and threw me down the stairs. As he came to hit me again, I caught his arm, drew him down to me and made him make love to me.

I carried this thought throughout the day, giving in to the sensation and pleasure as I've never done before.

Knowing that what I was thinking was wrong, I never called upon God for help.

My thoughts throughout the day were: "You will never feel a man's hands on you again, or feel a kiss upon your lips. God is a jealous God and wants you all to Himself. And once you say yes to Him, that You want only His love, He will abandon you and you will never feel His love again. He wants you to give Him everything, to come to Him and put everything about you under the house." [When I moved in with my husband, he had me put everything I possessed under the house. It hurt a very great deal for that was me that went under the house.]

Finally at the end of the day, I thought of God once again, of how I had offended Him throughout that whole day. I said, "OK, if that is what you want, God. I give it all to you. At least I am moving in with You with my eyes open. When I married, I did not know that is what a woman must do when she marries, but I will come to You, giving You everything. I have experienced Your love and that is all I want. I give this sin, these temptations to Jesus, to add to His love. For I cannot handle them alone."

I lay on the floor, crying, asking for His mercy, for the lustful thoughts I had had all day, when suddenly my tears stopped, a great peace came over me, and the thought came into my mind, "The Lord is with you. Go in peace, to love and serve the Lord."

Then I thought, "Oh, good! God has forgiven me my sins. I don't have to go to confession. I don't want my pastor to think anything bad of me. Of course, I could go to another priest." But I forced myself to go to my pastor Sunday night. He did not consider my temptations and my experience as sin. And Monday God loved me! I spent the day feeling my soul glowing red hot for love of God, and often in deep Rest.

In regards to this dream I have just described, I have no idea if it had religious symbolism or not. Perhaps it was a dream of interpreting dying to oneself as God killing me and in my desperation, my reaching out to Him to love me. My pastor said he doubted my dreams represented my real future, but rather revealed my deep, deep needs that any single person has.

I saw the two days as battles similar to those described by other contemplatives. Those thoughts I had were definitely Satan, trying to tempt me away from God. God had stepped aside for me to fight these fights alone.

My friend Carey interpreted the symbolism of my reaching up and grabbing the man's arm, as my grabbing the bad things of my life and not letting them control me any more.

I know that I was healed of many fears and hurts that day. I gave myself to God that day but I said that I wanted to keep my emotions and passions. These may be to me a source of constant struggle to control, but they are what makes me human. I am not divine. I am human. I may struggle to be like God, but I am still a human with all my weakness. I love God with all my humanness, including all my emotions and my passions.

I had yet another dream. This time I was in a very small building out in the middle of nowhere. The building was like a clubhouse children would build. It consisted of two rooms, each about 7 feet square. I was with a man who was all in white and I thought him to be an angel, although he did not have wings.

I left the clubhouse and went to a field where my ex-husband was working. I sat down at the edge of it and soon laid down. I looked up and there was my ex-husband kneeling by my side. He never stopped work for me before, even if I had been gone for several months. I felt this was a sign that, if I went back to him, everything would be different and he would love me and our marriage would be good.

I said, "Jesus Christ, son of the living God, have mercy upon me, a sinner," and then, "This is not what I want." I got up and left. I returned to the clubhouse. I went into the second room, removed all my clothes and put on a white garment. I went into the other room and stood before the angel and said, "I reject Satan and all his works and empty promises. I believe in God, the Father Almighty, creator of heaven and earth. I believe in Jesus Christ, his only Son...." [I was saying my Baptismal vows.]

It was suggested that this angel was not an angel but Jesus himself. This dream symbolized my marriage to Jesus.

I had yet a fourth dream. People were coming to my house all at the same time, and my house wasn't ready for them. [My house is never ready for company.] One person was a cousin of my cousin, "Mary". She

I HAD A DREAM

said she had come to check me out, for "Mary" believed what I had told her.

Another person came to rent my cabin, and when we went into the building, I noticed someone was living in my cabin without me knowing it. Everything was neat and orderly, not one thing was out of place. Pretty flowers were set about. Although someone was living in this cabin, it was kept ready to be rented.

In other words, my house was not ready for people to come, but my cabin had an unknown person living in it that kept it ready for those who were coming.

I gave this dream this interpretation: My house represents the outer me. It will never be ready, in my mind, perhaps for anything. I will always have more to learn, things to do, places to go and see, etc. But God's plan for me will start now, whether I feel I am ready for it or not.

My cabin represents my soul. The someone who is unknown who lives there is God. He has made the place beautiful and peaceful, ready in wait for whenever I withdraw into the inner me.

Perhaps it also means that the outer me will never be ready for giving testimony to God's presence in everyone's lives, but the Holy Spirit in my soul will supply me with the words, the courage to do so, in such a way as to help people accept and welcome the Word.

My image of God is of the Unknown God and that is why He would be depicted as such in my dream. If I say, "God is Love," just by saying those words and putting a label upon Him, limits Him for He is more than our finite understanding of Love. If I write, "G.O.D.", this act of writing limits Him for He is more that three letters.

Song of Hope

Our minds can not comprehend all that He is or can do.

When I was drawn into deep contemplative prayer, all thought, all feeling was gone. I knew I was with God, not at the moment, but before and afterwards. This "nothingness" that I experienced at the moment was God. I did not know what He was doing to me. I did not know what wisdom He was planting in my mind. I did not know anything at the time. So in my mind, He became the God of Unknown.

When I read the book, Cloud of Unknowing I recognized this as a description of my experience with God.

The four dreams ended that phase of my spiritual journey during which I learned to recognize and be healed of my barriers to being filled with the Holy Spirit, my barriers to accepting God's love within me.

The four dreams began the budding of new lessons and understanding of my relationship with Jesus. From this time on, I accepted Jesus as my spouse and my love. I took a private vow to remain single.

Eternal Father, lead us not into temptation. I unite my hurts, my pain, my suffering to that of Jesus. Please forgive those who have hurt me. Please forgive me for hurting others. Please heal me. Please be my strength during the times of trial and temptation, when I begin to doubt Your Word, Your promises to us. In You only, will I be victorious. Please help me die to my false self so that You can mold me to Your will, so that I may become one with You.

SONG OF HOPE

I was awakened in the night with the words of the first
sentence of this song of hope running through my mind.
It repeated itself continuously. Usually, if I awake in the
night with an idea I think, "If this is important, remind
me in the morning," and go back to sleep. But I couldn't
think this. I couldn't think any other thought. And so I
sat up, grabbed a note pad from my bedside stand and
wrote down the first sentence, which came to me as a
man's voice singing it, and I went back to sleep.

I awoke a second time with the second sentence
continuously running through my mind. I wrote it
down and went back to sleep.

I was awakened five times and wrote the following
poem. Unfortunately I did not try to figure out the tune
and I have forgotten how it was sung.

I do not consider myself to have the gift of prophecy,
but to me, it was Jesus singing me this song and it is for
the whole world "A Song of Hope."

I also gave my book this title, for I believe that
what I have recorded is a sign of hope for all the world.
If little ol' me, a divorcee, a single parent, a person who
stopped going to church, can experience this love of God,
then anyone can. God is holding each one of us in His
hand and is in each moment in our lives.

A few nights later I was awakened by a chorus of

voices singing the song "Gifts". This time, as I sat up to write the words, the song continued until I had it all down. I stopped the song after the phrase "To regard all things as beautiful, to set things free," and objected, "How can I set things free?" and the answer came, "Free from prejudice, free from hate..." And after the phrase "All Heaven and earth will sing glory to you," I asked, "What do you mean? Sing glory to me? There must be some mistake." And the choir then repeated these two verses as if to emphasize that I had heard them correctly. I believe that this was a choir of angels that sang this song. I sang the phrases, "I give You my hope, I give You my dreams," etc.

These gifts are not just for me but are given to all mankind.

SONG OF HOPE

In the goodness of the Lord
We seek His Presence.
In the goodness of the Lord
We know His Presence.

In the stillness of the Lord
We hear His voice.
In the love of the Lord
We know the Lord.

In the goodness of the Lord
All shall know Him.

4/16/94

GIFTS

The value of life
This is my gift to you.

To know Him and to love Him
These are my gifts to you.

Your sons, your family
These are my gifts to you.

All Heaven and earth,
All life to cherish
These are my gifts to you.

My Son
He is my gift to you.

To regard all things as beautiful
To set things free
These are my gifts to you.

(Free from prejudice, free from hate, free from
the hold of evil.)

113

Song of Hope

All Heaven and earth will sing glory to you
These are my gifts to you.

[I give You my hope, I give You my dreams,
I give You my life as a tool.
These are my gifts to You, Oh Lord,
These are my gifts to You.
I give You my life, I give You my love.
These are my gifts to You.]

To regard all things as beautiful
To set things free
These are my gifts to you.

All Heaven and earth will sing glory to you
This is my gift to you.

[My Lord and my God, You are too kind. I
do not deserve such a gift.
It is an honor and a privilege to receive such a
gift. And to live my life as Your tool.
My Lord and my God, I love You so much
This is my gift to You.]

4/27/94

MY FATHER, MY SPIRIT,
AND I LIVE WITHIN YOU

I was awakened by an extremely bright light. The words swooshing into my mind were, "My Father, my Spirit and I live within you."

What does this mean? This message was something new to me. I wasn't raised on such Catholic teaching. To have it come to me in the middle of the night, to suddenly understand and believe it and know it is true, is awesome.

I am still probing its meaning. These words were the first lessons taught to me, for understanding "The eternal incarnation of the Word within us."

John's gospel has become more meaningful to me. "And I will ask the Father, and he will give you another Advocate to be with you always...On that day you will realize that I am in my Father and you are in me and I in you." (John 14:16,20. N.A.B.)

Charismatics usually attribute every good they feel or experience to the Holy Spirit; but the whole Trinity, Father, Son, and Holy Spirit, dwell within us.

Two days after these words came into my mind, I opened the book, "Abandonment to Divine Providence" by Jean-Pierre de Caussade, to chapter III and began reading:

> Sometimes we live in God and sometimes
> God lives in us. These are very different

115

states. When God lives in us, we should abandon ourselves completely to him, but when we live in him, we have to take care to employ every possible means to achieve a complete surrender to him...

But when God lives in us, we have nothing to help us beyond what he gives us moment by moment. Nothing else is provided and no road is marked out. We are like a child who can be led about wherever one wishes and who is ignorant of everything except what is put in front of it. We are given no books with carefully marked passages, and very often we have no regular director, for God leaves us without any support except himself. We are abandoned and live in darkness...

God sees nothing better in us than this total resignation of ourselves, and he himself provides us with books, gives us insight into our souls, together with advice and examples from the lives of the good and wise...

They who live in God perform countless good works for his glory, but those in whom God lives are often flung into a corner like a useless bit of broken pottery. There they lie, forsaken by everyone but yet enjoying God's very real and active love and knowing they have to do nothing but stay in his hands and be used as he wishes. Often they have no idea how they will be used, but he knows...

MY FATHER, MY SPIRIT,
AND I LIVE WITHIN YOU

Whenever I think of loving God I feel the Presence of the Holy Spirit come over me. I call it the Presence of God's Love. God loves me and wants me to experience this love. All this is happening to me!

My friend, Carey, had a prophetic word for both of us: Jesus was within us both and His Love radiated from both of us. Together we acted as mirrors facing each other, reflecting His love infinitesimally. Then she saw this mirror as six faceted, again reflecting this love forever. We were also described as "The Valley" with many precious jewels soon to be found, uncovered. God was showering gifts on us, The Valley, never before used or imagined. We were "The Earth". And He was showering The Earth with Gifts. We will be God's instruments, setting people free, in such a way that people will know that it is from God, that He is behind it all. I will teach as never before, say things as never before, and people will know it is all from God.

After this prophecy, we discussed its meaning. The words, "Jesus was within us", and also, "to set people free", had been received by me earlier.

I had been given the song, "Gifts" and they were all gifts of Love — The value of life, my sons, my family, all life to cherish, to set things free.

About a month after this prophecy from Carey the "National Catholic Register" had an article entitled, "More than riches, power or fame, God is the ultimate object of our desire", and another subtitle, "A kingdom beyond our wildest dreams," June 6, 1994, page 1. The author, Father Jacob Restrick, O.P., compared the Kingdom of God to winning the sweepstakes. Some random quotes from the article include:

Song of Hope

We'd all agree that our lives would change ... In fact, that's just what the Kingdom of Heaven is: It's being made one with Christ and having His Life, His grace, His spirit in us. Jesus is the treasure beyond all treasures. Open up this treasure chest and you will find riches beyond your wildest wishes. In Him is divine Truth. He is Truth, the fullest and most perfect revelation of what our lives are about...

Jesus is the fullness of life and when He lives in you, your life changes....

(Sin) robs us of the treasure: the peace and joy of God's living presence and the gifts of the Holy Spirit...

How many people find the buried treasure of faith and keep it buried...

Only human beings have the capacity to desire infinite treasures: truth, beauty, love, union with God and eternal life. Only the human kingdom is capable of "finding" the Kingdom of God and knowing this is the only treasure that responds to the infinite desires of our heart.

Yes, our lives change when we truly embrace the faith, that marvelous "field" in which we possess the Lord. The "cost" is total surrender. The treasure chest, however, is infinitely deep and filled with drawers and compartments a lifetime can't fully uncover. To possess this treasure, this pearl beyond all others, you don't have to do anything - all you have to do is accept it.

I had the treasure right before my eyes but this article opened my eyes to see Jesus and the treasure He has given me. It is unimaginable, beyond all description. To read this article, to think these thoughts, and have a wave of God's love come over me, engulf me, embrace me with an awesome hug... brings tears to my eyes.

Over and over, after I am given a message, I come across an explanation in something I read. God knows the future. He teaches me. He knows that soon an explanation will be given to me. Shortly, my pastor will mention it in a sermon, or I will read the same idea in the Bible, or I will come across an article on the subject in a newspaper or book. I listen or read more attentively and the message sinks into me and becomes more a part of me. The message is God saying, "Pay attention! This is important. This I want you to know and understand."

I learn best through reading. God does not often give me immediate understanding of His messages. The meaning is often given to me by reading. God teaches us the way we learn the best.

After I receive a message, the understanding of it may come in my response to a question about this very same subject. Thus I am led by God to help others.

That is how God works in and with us.

God gives people experiences, not to be kept hidden in themselves, but to share with others. We need to take the time to sit in silence, to listen to God. God takes each of us, as we are, and communicates to us in ways we will accept. Since I am, by nature, a quiet introvert, I can write about finding God within me during silence. A talkative, active extrovert may have a hard time sitting in silence. She will have to give her testimony to how God has communicated to her through her paintings, through her dance, through her active prayer with others, through her looking into the eyes of the sick or the poor.

With this message, God began teaching me the meaning of the words, "Eternal Incarnation of the Word within us". This was the first of a new way of learning for me. This was the first lesson on this subject. The rest of this book will be on these lessons.

Eternal Father, guide me in the direction
You want me to go.
It is very frustrating, very trying, not to know what
You prefer me to do. You created all things. You
know all things. Help me to trust in You.

THE SCRIPT

In the chapter entitled, "Trust in the Lord" I related how I realized that I was a writer while listening to a self-improvement tape. That is what I am. I decided to quit my stressful job and go full time writing. When I went to a healing Mass a few days after this decision, I prayed that my mind would be cleared to think, that my hands would write. At the time, I thought only of myself. I did not think God would use my writing.

I had always dreamed of writing, but did not write. I kept that dream hidden deep inside me. When I got a divorce, all creativity died, including writing. The decision to go full time writing was a very major one.

I had worked with a friend, Jim Denny, compiling his family letters. These were letters written between 1860 and 1880, between the gold mining town of Callahan, California and Vermont. Both sides saved their letters. These letters when typed and double spaced comprised over 1000 pages. The various publishers liked the manuscript but encouraged us to publish it through a university press.

We could see that our manuscript could easily be turned into a movie or mini series. About this time the movie, "Dances with Wolves" was released. Jim could visualize Kevin Costner in the lead. While in Southern California he visited the studio where the movie was made and this studio asked to see the manuscript, the diaries, the local history book that I had written, photographs, everything we had. We said we were not script writers, but when they returned the materials they said they didn't have the time to turn this into a script, but if we did, they would consider it.

Jim, who was in his 70's, said he was too old to learn script writing but if I wanted to give it a try, he would give me the rights. I went to the library and got a book on everything one needs to know on writing a movie script. "I can do this." The golden ring was held out before me and I went for it. That was my goal when I decided to become a full time writer.

I had enough money to live for three years without an income.

For two years I worked on that script - well, I have already written saying what was also happening to me during this time. God was taking most of my thought time, but nearly every Friday I would sit down and crank out enough pages on the script to equal the average week's worth.

A script is written differently than a book. A script is written over and over, each time by expanding it, fleshing it out. I wrote two drafts, then joined a college class on acting, directing, play writing in order to develop the dialogue.

The students in the class would act out my work so I could see if they interpreted it the way I wanted. I could also see if the dialogue sounded real or not.

I also had to get on the stage and act and this helped me recognize what was crucial to be included in the script and what could be left for the interpretation by the director.

THE SCRIPT

My teacher praised my work, saying it was some of the best writing that had crossed her desk. I wrote a scene that she especially liked. "Send this to an actress and she will see a Tony in this," she said. "She will have her agent arrange all the details of it getting produced and she will hire you to finish the script." I planned on returning to the next class with it ready to mail out.

I was to act out this scene. I had it all memorized, but to my embarrassment, once on the stage I couldn't remember one line that I had written, not even after a prompt.

I went home that night bewildered. Why did my memory leave me? I could understand it if I was under stress, but there was only a handful of students in class that day, and I wasn't being graded. There was no stress.

The next day, sitting outside on my lawn chair, I recited the whole scene from memory without forgetting one word. I had a feeling God had something to do with my lack of memory.

The scene included cursing. I did not know much about it. I wondered if this offended God. I wondered, if when an actor cursed on stage, would this effect the actor that was being cursed? (My pastor assured me later that the Bible was filled with cursing, and such language was part of all great drama. You had to have people being bad to show their change toward good.)

That night I went to bed praying about the scene, asking God, if He was offended by the cursing, to please give me better words to use.

During the night I dreamed about this same prayer, when suddenly my tongue felt as if someone grabbed onto it. I didn't realize one moves their tongue during dreams, but my tongue wouldn't move. This sensation woke me up. When I was awake, a voice spoke into my thoughts, "Thy God has plans for thee. Do not submit this script."

I didn't.

I was very bewildered by this experience. If this message was from God, He did not direct me on what He did want me to do.

I went to my spiritual director. She said this was not the way God normally worked. He normally takes your talents which He has given you and works through them. He doesn't take away one thing and leave a void. She told me to ask God to give me confirmation on this subject within a month and to talk to my pastor about this.

I had told my pastor that if God gave me a message to do something, I would go to him before I did it. Now I went to him because God told me not to do something.

My pastor had the experience of being called to the priesthood with an audible voice, so he knew God does give direction in such a manner. He also told me to ask God to confirm this message within the month.

A month went by and I received no confirmation.

I returned to the computer - and it crashed. When I went to have it repaired, they said they had never seen a computer lose so many sectors all at once. That took several weeks to get repaired.

Then my new car began to have flat tires. Within one month I had four flat tires, a cylinder went out and the air conditioning went out. One doesn't have much time to write when you are at the repair garage.

In July I attended a retreat. I told the retreat master this tale and asked what I was supposed to do for God.

I ask God but all I get is, "Love me. Simply love me." The retreat master answered, "That is your directive. No matter what you do, it should be out of love for God. Begin with your writing."

Two weeks after the retreat the director of "Friday Night with Jesus Ministries" asked me to write for their newsletter. I was so excited I sent him several months' worth of articles and he phoned and asked me to put my experiences in book form. And that is how this book came to be.

My Lord, my God. HELP!!!

SILENCE THAT PARALYZES

I went on a good old-fashioned week-long silent retreat. It was held at a Sisters of Mercy convent. I originally signed up for a retreat on the mystics, but this one was canceled. I had to choose another.

The events leading up to this retreat, the retreat itself, and the lessons following the retreat, became very important in my spiritual journey and growth into the Lord. God began teaching me in a different manner than previously.

There were several retreats offered. Each followed a different theme. One that interested me was on prayer. Another was on Thomas Merton. I had read several of Merton's books. I felt God had led me into my own form of contemplative prayer and He had led Merton on his own spiritual journey. So, I thought I did not really need instructions on either prayer or on Merton. My life was already one of silence and solitude. I did not feel the need for a retreat to "find" myself or give myself the time to relax.

Why was I going? How do I decide which retreat to take? I began to pray.

I am not used to praying before I act. I usually hear something and go for it, and as an after thought, ask God, if He disagrees, to interrupt my plans. In this case, I wanted to go on a retreat, but did not know why nor which one I would benefit from most.

I prayed, "Lord, what do You want me to take?"

How would God let me know? This was something new to me. "Lord, let me know by having the Holy Spirit come over me when I go over the options.... The retreat on prayer?" I felt nothing. "The retreat on Merton?" I felt nothing. "All of the above?" Nothing. "None of the above?" Nothing.

My conclusion from this prayer method (rightly or wrongly) was that God didn't care which one I took.

The next day I still had not made a decision. I was to call the convent and let them know my choice. I went out to my Mary's garden to pray again. As I sat before the statue of Our Lady of Guadalupe, immediately the Presence of the Holy Spirit came over me. I prayed, "Lord, I am trying to discern Your preferred will for me and I need the help of the Holy Spirit to instruct me. What should I do? I want the experience of a retreat. A silent one. Should I go to the one on prayer or the other one?"

After some mind searching I remembered the name, Thomas Merton.

"Lord, I have been told that solitary prayer is one thing, but I would like the experience of community prayer. I want to join my prayer with the rest on the retreat. Should I go to the one on prayer or the other one?"

Again, I had to think for awhile before I remembered the name, Thomas Merton.

"Lord, I promised myself to consider seriously convent life. I want that experience, plus a time to see if in some way I can discern Your call for me. Should I go to the one on prayer, prayer, prayer, (the word continuously came to my mind) or the other one?"

Song of Hope

This time I did not even try to recall the name, Thomas Merton, but phoned the convent and told them I wished to attend the retreat on prayer.

The Presence of the Holy Spirit left me as soon as I made the decision. It seemed to me that I made the decision on the basis of what I wanted. I have a hard time believing that what I want may also be what God wants.

A week before I left, I felt Jesus' sorrow. It was like holding a child on your lap who is crying. Perhaps his blanket is lost. You can feel the child's love for you and their sorrow. You feel sad, for the child is sad. You do not feel sad over the lost blanket, for it is not your loss. If you take the child and set him on the bench beside you, and close your eyes so that you no longer see the child and you close your ears so that you no longer hear the child, you can still feel his presence, his need and his sorrow. If the child slipped off the bench, you would know he was gone. If he returned and stood near you, you would know he was back.

That was how I felt the presence of Jesus, His love and His sorrow. St. Teresa of Avila, a doctor of the Catholic Church and one of the leading mystics of the church, in chapter 27 of The Book of Her Life, translated by Kavanaugh and Rodrigues, describes this type of vision. She wrote, "I saw nothing with my bodily eyes, or with my soul, but it seemed to me that Christ was at my side. I saw that it was He, in my opinion, who was speaking to me."

She called this type of vision an intellectual vision.

When I "felt" the sorrow of Jesus, I did not think of all the evil in the world nor imagine how Jesus felt and thus felt sorrowful myself. I felt His sorrow. St.

128

Teresa wrote:

> *It is incorrect to think that the vision is like*
> *that experience of those who are blind or in the*
> *dark who do not see the other at their side.*
> *There is some likeness to this comparison but*
> *not a great deal, because in such a case these*
> *people experience with their senses: either they*
> *hear the other person speak or stir, or they touch*
> *them. In the vision there is nothing of this, nor*
> *do you see darkness; but the vision is represent-*
> *ed through knowledge given to the soul that is*
> *clearer than sunlight.*

She also wrote, "Those who don't have a very living faith will be unable to believe in them."

I felt this sorrow so strongly, I cried for an hour, telling Him that I loved Him and that many, many people loved Him. Finally I got on the phone — there is nothing like being a fool for Jesus — and asked my friends and relatives, "Could you please say, "Jesus, I love You" just as many times as you possibly can for the rest of the day so that we can send up a huge wave of love to Him. We all need hugs, and today Jesus needs one."

The day before I left for the retreat, I laid down on the couch to take a nap. I thought, "Here I am, alone in this house and I am grinning from ear to ear. I am so happy I could burst!" The joy within me could not be contained. It was awesome!

A little while later, as I was packing, I felt Jesus' joy. I compare it to a feeling I had as I talked to a friend on a phone. She had a secret, a surprise for me and she was bursting with happiness. Even though I couldn't see her on the phone, I could still feel her happiness. I could not see her body language but I could feel her joy in the secret that she had for me.

Although I could not see Jesus, I felt Him beside me. I felt His happiness and that he had a secret, a surprise for me on this retreat.

The thought came to me that this silent retreat was going to be a honeymoon with Jesus. I never had this idea before. I did not read this. No one ever told me of such a concept. This idea just suddenly entered my thought process.

On a honeymoon, you sit, perhaps on the beach, nestled in each other's arms, not saying a word, just soaking up the feeling of love each has for the other. This became my concept of a silent retreat. Whenever you talk, you establish a relationship with the person you are talking with. On a silent retreat you deepen a relationship with Jesus.

Another thing happened before this retreat. I went to sleep and dreamed I was pruning flowers. I awoke and realized God was going to prune me. I had been praying, "You are the potter, I am the clay. Mold me and meld me and do with me what You will." But pruning is different. Pruning involves pain. Perhaps cutting away good wood as well as bad. Shortly afterwards I read in a book that pruning involves getting rid of faults and sins. Getting rid of dead wood that is not producing fruit.

I arrived at the convent. As a friend gave me a tour of the grounds, I felt the Presence of the Holy Spirit everywhere we went, but it was especially strong in the small chapel and at Mary's grotto. During dinner the feeling of the Presence became very strong and I felt Jesus say to me, "Oh, how I love these women! They have given their whole lives to me."

The third day, as I was eating lunch, I was thinking how wonderful it was that I didn't have to prepare this meal myself, and that I did not have to eat this meal by myself. How awful that every day of my life I eat alone.

Suddenly these pleasant, thankful thoughts turned into the feeling of loneliness and then...I recalled the last year of my marriage in which my husband refused to speak to me.

This pain sliced my heart — a paralyzing thought. All joy, all peace, all happiness seemed to vanish. This pain invaded all thought, all feeling. The silence suddenly became a fear! I wanted out of there!

Just as one who is afraid of heights from a rickety step ladder transfers this fear to all heights, even a safe mountain road, so too, this thought of silence took over. The atmosphere at the convent was one of silence. The feeling of love was still there. The other retreatants nodded and smiled as they passed me. This safe silence suddenly turned into menacing fear! I wanted out of there! Fortunately, I had caught a ride with a friend to the retreat, for if I had my car, I would have left.

I yelled at Jesus in my thoughts, "Jesus! This is our honeymoon! How could You do this to me? How could You bring up this hurtful memory and allow this tremendous fear! How dare You! If this is Your idea of a joyful surprise, forget it!"

Then I realized I would be healed! This was indeed the surprise He had for me.

If this was my second marriage and I was on a honeymoon with a human person, there would certainly be some incident that would bring up a memory of my past. That is part of life. My human partner would not be able to heal me of this hurt. Only God could do that.

I kept my mouth firmly shut, for if I opened it, sobs would come out. My eyes glistened with held-back tears.

My friend saw me in the hall in the evening. She asked how it was going. I could only shake my head. She saw the tears in my eyes. Knowing this was my first silent retreat she asked, "Is it the silence?"

I nodded yes.

"I'm on my way to the large chapel. I'll pray for you," she whispered.

I went into the small chapel. This room, once a library, was long and rectangular. One wall was all window. An altar was in the middle and the tabernacle to the left of it. Along the left wall was a baby grand piano which extended to a few feet from the tabernacle. About five rows of seats stretched across the room. Fresh bouquets of flowers stood in front of the tabernacle and in the middle of the altar.

I went to the farthest corner from the tabernacle, to the back right corner of the room.

"Eternal Father," I prayed, "I offer this hurting memory, to You, for the greater honor and glory of Your name and I give it to Your Son, Jesus, to add to His Love."

The next words were hard to say. "Please forgive my ex-husband. Please help me to forgive him."

"Please, take away this pain! Please comfort me. Heal me, please!"

Thoughts boiled into me, "If God was calling you to a religious life, it would be one of silence. You think this is bad! In religious life its paralyzing fear will be a hundred times worse! God will take away His Love. You will no longer feel it. You will be alone. All alone."

Such thoughts tormented me!

The next words were extremely hard to say. "OK.
If that is God's will, so be it. If I experience such hurtful
silence again, so be it."

I had two tissues in my pocket. My tears filled
them both. I began looking around the room for more.
Not seeing any, I thought maybe there were some behind
the piano.

As I approached the tabernacle, the Power of the
Presence of God engulfed me. A voice spoke within me,
"Come, sit, and abide in Me."

I sat and was instantly wrapped within God's
Love! I felt it flow around me and through me. It felt as
if I was nestled within a blanket of security and held in
Jesus' arms. Such love! Such joy! Such peace! I could
not move, nor did I want to. I sat there, in stillness and
silence, soaking up God's love.

I remained thus for over an hour.

I left the chapel with a smile on my face. I could
now talk about the past without crying. The memory was
not taken away, only the pain of it.

This was His surprise and Gift to me, a wonderful
healing.

I told the experience to the retreat master, who
summarized my story: "You were given a hurt memory.
You asked for intercessory prayer. You joined in union
with others for prayer. You asked God to help you forgive.
You asked Him to heal you and comfort you. You had
temptations trying to pull you away from God. You
went seeking tissues, which represents the materialistic
world. You felt the Presence of God. You heard God's

plea, "Come, sit, and abide in Me." You responded. You experienced His overwhelming Love and He healed you. A very healthy spiritual experience."

In a capsule, that is how God heals. Sometimes in this healing process, we suffer. In the past, I would have taken this painful memory, relished the hurt, adding to my bitterness toward men, my hatred toward authority figures, and remained a broken, hurting person. I could have spent hundreds of dollars seeing a counselor, trying to recall the hurts in my life and then, perhaps, not been healed. Jesus heals us freely. His love and healing are free. Come to Him. Take one step toward Him, and He will run to you.

The healing of memories is a never ending cycle. We must learn to forgive those close to us and then extend this forgiveness to the whole world.

The retreat master spoke to us for forty-five minutes twice a day. The rest of the time we had to ourselves to be spent in silence. I wrote the thoughts that came to me. When I returned to hear the retreat master, his subject was always on what I had just written! He confirmed what I had been taught by Jesus about prayer. At the end of the week he told us that this retreat had been unprepared. Try as he would, he could not think of what to say until he entered our meeting room.

Jesus opened my mind to our relationship throughout my whole life. I recalled prayers that were answered. I realized that hardships I went through and heartaches I experienced had formed me into the person I am. I realized Jesus had been in and with me throughout it all. He put friends into my life when I needed them. He was behind the "good luck" or the coincidences which occurred.

This lesson was reinforced by a trip to Wisconsin a few weeks after this retreat. I was shown how God works within people's lives. It was a vacation planned and given to me by God. I write about this vacation in a later chapter.

I had two visions on this retreat. Both were images projected on the back of my eyelids, behind my closed eyes. I saw two huge candles held out over the water. The candles were like the Statue of Liberty which signifies freedom. This vision signified the Freedoms given through Christ Jesus. His Light shows the way to water and freedoms. Through Jesus we become free from prejudice, from hate, from the hold of evil. The water represents Baptism, the Holy Spirit, Graces given by God. The arms holding the two candles were my own.

In the second vision a man held a chalice for me to drink. I just saw the torso of this man, wearing priestly vestments, and I heard, "Come, drink my blood."

The meaning of this vision was not clear to me at first. I pondered it and opened my Bible to see if I could discern its meaning from Scripture. Amazingly I quickly found various passages and each one revealed a deeper meaning in these words, "Come, drink my blood."

From Mark 14:22-24 I learned that when we drink His blood we enter a new community or life with Christ. Matt 26:26-28 says blood is the source of life. His blood is for the forgiveness of sins. The Blood of Jesus is the Gift of Forgiveness.

Mark 10:38-40 asks us to drink this cup, i.e., to accept the destiny assigned or sanctioned by God. We are asked to share in the sufferings of Jesus, the endurance of tribulations and suffering for the gospel.

1 Cor 11:26 says that when we drink the cup we proclaim the death of the Lord. It is an action of self-giving and the command, "Drink this cup", is to repeat His action.

Realize what we are doing! Grasp and internalize the meaning of Jesus' death before eating and drinking the cup. Perceive the imperative for unity. Jesus gives Himself to all.

The cup being offered means having been tested, we have been found true. Suffering, trials and tribulations are not over until Jesus returns in full glory.

Accepting the cup means OK, I realize this.

The blood is the Eucharist. We take it and then go out into the world with what we have received. We are His hands, His feet, His body.

Lord Jesus Christ,
I offer to you this situation that has surfaced in my
memory. Help me forgive. Please, heal me of hurts.
And if it should happen again, help me endure it.

AID ME

Aid me in loving You, my Lord.
Beautify me with Your love.
Burn me with Your love.
Catch me in Your love and never let me go.
Cleanse me with Your love.
Comfort me with Your love.
Drench me with Your love.
Enlighten me with Your love.
Fill me with Your love.
Grant me the gift of loving You.
Guide me with Your love.
Heal me with Your love.
Hide me in Your love.
Inebriate me with Your love.
Jesus, I love You. Help me love You more.
Justify me with Your love.
Kindle within me the fire of Your love.
Lead me with Your love.
Melt the chain which closes my heart to Your love.
Mold me and meld me with Your love.
Nestle me in Your cocoon of love.
Open Your heart for me to enter into Your love.
Open my heart to receive Your love.
Pour Your love upon me.
Prune me with Your love.
Purify me with Your love.

Song of Hope

Quicken my steps to embrace Your love.
Rid me of my false self through Your love.
Saturate me with Your love.
Slash away my fears with Your love.
Take me into Your heart with Your love.
Thank You for Your love.
Tie me to You forever with Your love.
Until the end of time, let me feel Your love.
Vest me in the armor of Your love.
Wrap me tightly in the comforting stillness of Your love.
Xtract from me all barriers to being completely filled with Your love.
Your love, Your Love, Your love is all I want.
Zap me with Your love.

RELATIONSHIP WITH JESUS

My life changed when I was Baptized in the Spirit. I call this my born again experience. Jesus entered my life more fully and became more real. I mark the beginning of our closer, fuller relationship as May 17. A few years after I was Baptized in the Spirit I had this experience:

In June, a few days after the Feast Day of St. John the Baptist, I had a vision. This vision was behind my closed eyes, projected upon the back of my eyelids. It was an image of a Saint. The words, "St. John the Baptist" came into my mind. I believed these identifying words came from God and as soon as they came into my mind, the image was gone. It was followed by another image, one of Christ ascending into Heaven.

I did not know what these two images signified. I thought that since it was shortly after the Feast Day of St. John the Baptist, I was supposed to ask this Saint to pray for me and so I did from that day on.

In August I went to Wisconsin. While there, circumstances brought me to my hometown on Sunday morning for Church.

The church building of my childhood had been replaced. It had been some eighteen years since I had last been in the new building.

Behind the altar, hung a cross; but instead of the crucified Jesus upon it, it contained the figure of Christ ascending into Heaven. It was the same image I had received in my vision.

The name of the church is St. John the Baptist.

As these thoughts came into my mind, I felt the strong Presence of the Holy Spirit come over me. I said, "Speak, Lord, for your servant is listening." And into my thoughts came these words:

"This is the church where you were baptized. This is where you made first confession and received first communion. This is where you were confirmed. This is where our relationship began."

My own thoughts continued, "And not three years ago when you were Baptized in the Spirit." I noticed that the thoughts also did not say, "From all eternity I knew you."

I was not given instant insight into this message. I read, I listened, I learned as much as I could about what Baptism means. The key words here are "Baptism" and "relationship began". Yes, God knows us from all eternity. He manifested His love for me when I was Baptized in the Spirit. But our relationship began when I was baptized. I had many questions. Would I have experienced the Manifestation of God's love if I had never been Baptized? That I will never know, for God manifests His love to everyone. Again, the key word is relationship.

To put things in their chronological order, I had the visions of the saint and Christ Ascending to Heaven in June. In July I went on the Six Day Silent Retreat. In August I went to Wisconsin. From the retreat onward, God began bringing into my memory my relationship with Him throughout my life.

With the simple act of writing J.M.J. at the top of all my papers for Jesus, Mary, Joseph, and praying over tests and my homework, I was within a relationship with Jesus.

My parents started me with this relationship. They were Catholics and we went to Mass each Sunday and sat together as a family. I went to Catechism and also to a Catholic school. We said the rosary, prayed and sang religious songs together. Although the subject of religion and spirituality seldom came up, I was taught respect for the church and the commandments. They taught me to pray and helped my relationship with Jesus.

To this very day, I remember my older brother and sister helping me prepare for first confession. With glee they pointed out all my sins. At the age of seven I realized that sin offended God and I promised my best never to offend Him. They helped me maintain this relationship with Jesus.

There were many hurting events, many nasty things said to me by religious people in the name of religion, many misleading instructions taught by church leaders during the 50's. God gave me grace to see beyond these as not being or sounding right. His grace made me realize these were people-things, and not of God. There will always be weeds among the wheat. I stepped into this realization, became rooted in it, and grew.

When I went to college, I went to Utah State University and the pastor and Newman chaplain there was Monsignor Jerome Stoffel. I became a Monsignor Catholic. He said the Mass so reverently, so devotedly. His sermons hit everyone there. Each person felt that the words were directed straight at them. Monsignor was an intellectual. If he could believe all that the church taught, then so would I.

Song of Hope

I believed God acted through this man in his teaching. My boyfriend and I had a big discussion on the Catholic Church while upstairs in the Newman Club library. He had many questions I could not answer, for I barely knew my faith. That evening we attended a class Monsignor offered. Only one other person showed up, so Monsignor just talked and answered every single one of my boyfriend's questions. I knew that either Monsignor had an open intercom into the Library or else God spoke to us through him. I believed the latter.

I was attracted to this priest's spirituality. I attended daily Mass and listened attentively to every thing he said, hoping to understand and grow in my faith. Since I had become attached to God through the faith of another person, I did not think my faith very strong or even important.

Almost 90% of my prayers were answered, and I became very careful of what I prayed for; but I did not think of myself as having a good relationship with Jesus. If any big problem came up, I took it to Monsignor and asked for his prayers. Whether I realized it not, the relationship was there and becoming more deeply rooted.

I got married and many, many of my prayers were answered. As a child I had dreamed of living on a ranch in the West, having horses, and having two sons. I received all these. My boys were 18 months apart and quite a handful. When one was asleep, the other was awake. I was tired, but also unhappy and depressed. It was so easy to take out my frustration on these defenseless children. God gave me grace to realize what I was doing. I prayed to become the mother He wanted me to be, and I prayed especially to the Virgin Mary, the Mother of God, to treat and behave with my children as she would. I prayed to be given enough sleep and not to be so tired. This prayer was answered. From that day on, I always received a nap or else an all night sleep. When my eldest son was a teenager, he said to me that he was glad of the way I raised him, for people respected him. This was heavenly music to my ears. This was a confirmation that my prayer had been answered.

Every human relationship has a beginning or introduction. Baptism is that introduction. It is more than just something done with a newborn baby. Baptism must be taken seriously. Otherwise it becomes like a marriage in which you never meet your spouse. Parents who never teach their baptized children who Jesus is, are doing just that. They are leaving their children to meet Him by happenstance. They are denying them a whole life time to become rooted within this relationship.

Shortly after I was Baptized in the Holy Spirit I was given the prophecy, "I have planted you firmly and deeply in the ground. You will grow higher than the highest Cedar of Lebanon, taller than the tallest palm." Several years later I found these words in the Bible under the 92nd Psalm. In this psalm, instead of ground, it says, "planted in the temple of the Lord". He plants us in the temple of his church through Baptism. Only by taking this sacrament seriously will we become rooted in our relationship.

Dear Lord,
I want our relationship to grow. Please teach me.

A VACATION GIVEN BY GOD

The dream depicting my death, that I wrote about in the chapter, "I had a Dream", I believed, predicted my own physical death. If I were to die soon, I reasoned, I should visit my family, so, I made plans to go to Wisconsin.

This vacation trip, I believe, was given to me by God. In all His wisdom, He knew how I would interpret this dream.

As soon as Dad learned that I wanted to come home, he sent me money for the plane fare. I had already announced to my family that I was coming home and the check was in the mail before I had the interpretation from my friend Carey that the dream meant a spiritual death to one's false self.

Shortly after I announced I was coming to Wisconsin, I received a phone call. The person identified herself as "Mary". She was compiling a genealogy and had discovered writing on the back of an old photograph of a relative, giving the name of a town in Wisconsin. She drove to that town and looked up the family name in the phone book. The man she chose to call on, said they couldn't possibly be relatives. He had a copy of my family history book, "Roses in December", lying on the kitchen table. Mary opened the book and there under her finger was her ancestor's name. The two hugged and rejoiced over finding new relatives.

As Mary and I talked, we discovered we shared common ancestors five generations back. She was excited to learn that I was coming to Wisconsin and offered to drive me anywhere I wanted to go.

"There is someplace I'd like to go," I said.

"Name it. I'll drive you there."

"I'd like to go to Minnesota."

"I'll drive you there."

"This is clear across Wisconsin and half way across Minnesota."

"I'll drive you there."

"This is to a convent. I'd like to visit a friend there."

"I'll drive you there."

I wanted to visit a Benedictine nun to whom I had been writing all my religious experiences ever since they happened. We met twenty some years ago. When I was an undergraduate at Utah State University she was working on her doctorate. We had kept in touch over the years especially at Christmas time. When these religious experiences began, I wanted to talk to someone, to confirm I wasn't crazy.

At the end of my Christmas letter, I wrote one little sentence. Although it was sent to everyone, it was written especially for my Benedictine friend to see if she would understand. I wrote, "This year God touched me. Personally, physically. He engulfed me in Love, Peace. He took away all fear, all pain. I pray that He touches each and every one of you."

If she understood what I wrote, I knew I could confide in her.

Various people wrote back mentioning that sentence,

saying things like, "We're glad you are happy." But Sister wrote back saying how wonderful that I was being showered with God's graces. She said just the right words and in a few days she received a fifteen page letter from me and has continued to do so every month since then. She became my confidant.

In my letters to her, I sorted out my thoughts and experiences and often their meaning came to light as I wrote. Since she didn't know anyone involved, nor would she ever meet them, I wrote freely of my friends and their spiritual growth. I cried out my soul to her when some of my friends literally turned their backs to me, calling me satanic. She was a sounding board, not a spiritual director, and her letters to me were very short but filled with the Holy Spirit. When I reread them, I am filled with the Presence of the Holy Spirit, and thus I know He guided her pen.

And so my cousin "Mary" entered my life and through her I was able to visit Sister.

In Wisconsin, whenever I met someone, I felt the Presence of the Holy Spirit come over me and the words, "How I love this person," flooded my thoughts. When you meet people with the thought of how much Jesus loves them, you can't help meeting them with this love flowing from you. And they showered me with love in return. People were so good to me. They went out of their way to give me a good time.

I was given the awareness of Jesus' love for them. I did not know how the person felt. Many times I went into homes without one religious article in them and learned the people never prayed or attended church. How sad it must be for Jesus to carry on this one way relationship of love. They lived a good life but they lacked the friendship of a person wanting to be their friend.

I met very religious people of various religions. Some opened up to me and told me stories they had never told another person before, of God's Presence in their lives, of God's healing, and love.

One of the Virgin Mary's messages given at Medjugorje is that God honors all religions. People have made the divisions.

When I went to the Benedictine convent in Minnesota, Sister told me that every morning in her prayer she asks God what she should do that day. This day came the message, "Be nice to Kathy."

I do not take lightly messages from God. This simple message was given to Sister and related to me for a reason. Sister would naturally be nice to me. I was her guest and friend. Why would God give her this message?

Everyone on this vacation had been extremely nice to me. I was showered with love. I realized they had all received this message in their thoughts. God was teaching me that He works through our thought processes and we can listen or not, attribute the ideas to Him or not.

He awakes us on Sunday morning and gives us the thought there is church today. We are free to say, "I'm too tired," and go back to sleep.

By conversing and nurturing a closer relationship with God (praying) we can more easily listen, and learn to recognize His directives and illumination. We can also ignore Him and fail or shut Him out, and refuse to recognize Him. Some live completely in darkness.

We do not become robots by listening to and heeding God's voice. We can choose to be guided by it or not. We learn, through trial and error, that it is best to choose to follow the voice guiding us toward good, and thus, connect our will with God's. A soldier learns the same lesson. He learns it is for his best interest and the common good to obey instantly the directive of his commanding officer.

I've already written about the visions coming true in my home town church and the message given to me that our relationship with God as His children, living in His life, starts with our Baptism. I want to stress that the key word here is "relationship", for God is in us from the point of conception. But not as graced children of God, sharing God's personal life. St. Teresa of Avila described it as a light within us, as a lantern. When we sin, a dark veil comes over this light. As we continue to turn away from God, which is what sin is, the light gets fainter and fainter and soon all is dark. It takes a long time to cover this light, a long time of hurts and pain and unforgiveness and turning away from and rejecting God, and His love and forgiveness. It takes only a second to turn to God, say and sincerely mean you are sorry, and have the light begin to shine again.

God welcomes us the moment we say yes. It may be a long time to get over hurts and our patterned behavior, but God accepts us where we are and is patient as we struggle. Oh, would that we humans were as patient with each other!

I returned to California anxious to tell my pastor what I experienced. He only had a half hour free and I talked as fast as I could. As I was finishing, I followed him to his car and stood by the car door, still jabbering away. I had spouted out a very condensed version.

Father said, as he started the engine, "That's the eternal Incarnation of the Word within you."

What did this mean?

When finally I had a minute with Father again, I said, "I want to talk some more about "The eternal Incarnation of the Word within you."

Father said, "What does that mean?"

I knew then that this was another lesson by the Holy Spirit. He spoke through my pastor to me.

God is everywhere, in us, around us and through us. Charismatics learn the power of the Holy Spirit. But often, we are less conscious of the entire Trinity. God the Father, God the Son, and God the Holy Spirit, one God, one nature of three divine persons. They cannot be separated. Where one is, they all are.

My message in the night, "My Father, my spirit, and I live within you" confirms this reality.

In John 14: 16-21, 23 in the New American Bible, Jesus is quoted as saying,

I will ask the Father and he will give you another Advocate to be with you always, the Spirit of truth, which the world cannot accept, because it neither sees nor knows it. But you know it, because it remains with you and will be in you. I will not leave you orphans; I will come to you. In a little while the world will no longer see me, but you will see me, because I live and you will live. On that day you will realize that I am in my Father and you are in me and I in you.

Whoever has my commandments and observes them is the one who loves me. And

whoever loves me will be loved by my Father,
and I will love him and reveal myself to him.
    Whoever loves me will keep my word,
and my Father will love him, and we will come
to him and make our dwelling with him.

God is Love. God loves His son eternally, and His son is eternally loving His Father. The Holy Spirit is this love. And we are involved in this divine life, receiving this love, being saturated with this love, vibrating with this love, even though we are finite creatures of limited capacity.

Mary's messages from Medjugorje, emphasize conversion over and over again. She doesn't mean by conversion to become a Catholic. She means turn toward God, accept Him into your life, every day, continuously, forever. One definition of eternal is perpetual, ceaseless, endless, no beginning, no end, no limitations. I think that is what this means in "eternal incarnation of the Word within us." By continuously accepting Jesus into our lives, by saying, "Let me be your hands, your feet, your voice in this world," Jesus is being reincarnated or birthed eternally within us.

During the following Easter vigil service on Holy Saturday, as I watched people being received into the Catholic church and Baptized, I recalled my dream of a year before of standing before Jesus in my white baptismal gown and reciting to Him my baptismal promises, which in my dream signified my marriage to Him.

I realized I did not know this Jesus as a spouse and I could not accept this image. I did not have a good concept of marriage to bring into this notion of marriage with Jesus.

A VACATION GIVEN BY GOD

Easter Sunday brought no joy. I felt empty.

The following week, while meditating upon the scripture verse (John 20: 14) about Mary of Magdala not knowing or recognizing Jesus in his present, risen form, I realized that I did not recognize Jesus in my life in His present form.

When I went to Mass on Sunday a strange, most wonderful feeling came over me. "Strange" meaning an awareness I had never experienced before. A great CALM settled over me.

I wrote to my Benedictine friend about this awareness and tried to describe it. I realized that the martyrs must have had such a feeling before they died, and I prayed that if I had to die for my faith, that I, too, be given such an awareness. I typed the letter on my computer and wrote that it felt as if I was enveloped in TRUTH. I typed that word TRUTH and stopped. Truth? Why did I type that word, yet I could not think of a better one and so I left it.

On the very day I mailed this letter to Sister, I received one from her. She had asked her spiritual director how one knows if the "messages" one gets, come from Jesus, the devil, or one's own imagination. The director replied, "Ask if it is the Truth, for if it is the truth, it comes from Jesus, for Jesus is Truth."

As I read those words, I knew this great calm within me was indeed the Truth. I was aware of Jesus, of His present mode of being within us.

Jesus Christ, son of the Living God, help me love you. Help me keep your word. Help me believe in you.

WHAT DO YOU WANT ME TO DO?

The more I love God, the more I want to do something for Him. I want to live my whole life for Him. What does He want me to do?

I was given the message not to submit my script but I was never given something to take its place. I felt God wanted me to do something. Usually, I thought, people "love" you when they want something from you. I struggled with the truth that God loves me simply because He is love. He doesn't have any other reason. His love is absolute, benevolent and unconditional, and I cannot ever do anything to earn or merit this love. All I need to do is recognize it and accept it gratefully and live as if I believed in it.

I have been showered with love. I cannot receive all this love and keep it within me. I want to respond gratefully to God and share it with others. I will go any-where and do anything, if He but let me know what it is He prefers me to do. My message had been, "Thy God has plans for thee. Do not submit this script." I begged to be told these plans.

I posed this question to a retreat master. "I keep asking God, what do you want me to do? And in my thoughts, the phrase keeps coming, "Love me. Simply love me." The Retreat Master answered, "You've been given the answer. You have been given the Gift of Love for God. What ever you do, must manifest this love. Begin with your writing."

I went to the church and prayed again, "God, what do you want me to do?" The words of Mary came into my mind, "Do what ever He tells you." I protested in frustration, "But that is what I'm asking! I don't know what He is telling me to do!"

The words, "Do what ever He tells you," just kept repeating in my mind.

I recalled that Mary said these words at a wedding feast. To whom did she say them? The servants. What did they do? Filled the water jugs with water. And then they became the witnesses. They did not change the water into wine. They were merely the witnesses. I am the servant. I am to write. I am to fill with water the people who are thirsty. Whether my writing has an influence upon someone is not up to me or my style or way of writing. The Holy Spirit within a person will change them or not; will change the water of my words into the wine of love for Jesus. I am the servant. I am to write, to teach. This is the Gift the Holy Spirit has given me: Teaching. I should accept it, receive it as my own, develop it, live it. I should not say, "I am not good enough. Who will listen to or believe me? I will write and teach about God's love. Who will read it? Who will accept it? Who will be changed by it? That is not up to me. If it happens, I am the witness. But I do not do the changing. That will be between the person and God.

When Carey was praying over me, I was given a prophetic word. "You have planted something. It is not because you alone are a planter that this was planted. It is because of who you are in the divine sower who enabled you to plant."

I took these words into my own self. I wrote a book, not because I alone am a writer. It is who I am in the divine writer who enabled me to write. It is the divine "I AM" within me who enables me to do things. The divine "I AM" within me can free me from all barriers, and nurture, develop me into the best I can be.

This is a continuous process and is the eternal incarnation of the Word within us. It is also the way of being able to do whatever He tells us to.

Jesus Christ, Son of the Living God,
send your Holy Spirit and enable me
to accept the Gifts you have for me.

SACRAMENT OF THE SICK

*This Sacrament of the Sick, Sacrament of
Healing, Sacrament before death. We often
think of this Sacrament to be for the old and
the infirm....But OH, what healing God brings
about!*

*God heals us. He takes away physical
pain and begins to heal us.*

He heals us of the sickness...

> *Of physical ailments.*
> *Of unforgiveness.*
> *Of sinning against others.*
> *Of not caring about God.*
> *Of not caring about our souls.*

He heals us of brokenness...

> *Of broken hearts,*
> *Of stabs in the back,*
> *Of cruel comments which build*

*within us barriers limiting us from being our
whole selves.*

He heals us and forgives us.

He heals us enabling us to forgive others.

*He takes away the pain of hurting
memories*

of the past.
He takes away the immobilizing fear of
  the future.

It truly is the Sacrament before death...
  Death to false selves.
  Death to our selfish ways.
  Death to our clinging to material possessions.
  Death to our worry of what others
    think of us.

This Sacrament makes us alive...
  With Love,
  With wholeness,
  With awareness of the
    Presence of Jesus in us.

This Sacrament makes us free...
  Free from prejudice,
  Free from hate,
  Free from the hold of evil,

  This Sacrament is for everyone, not just for
those with major or minor physical needs but
for everyone who needs to be made whole again.

  Everyone.

THE DEATH OF BRUTUS

Brutus came with the house. He was a huge dog, his back came to my waist, but he was as gentle as could be. As a puppy they attempted to call him Fifi, but the name just wouldn't stick.

We'd go for walks every day, either crossing the river and following a mountain trail or else into town 1 1/2 miles away. Dogs would charge us, barking, defending their front yards, until they came close. Most could walk right under Brutus without their back touching his stomach. Dogs and my cats trusted him. His presence kept the deer and neighboring cats out of the yard. In his gentleness he ruled the neighborhood.

I regarded this big gentle dog as one of my gifts from God. He was my constant companion on walks. If I wanted to walk to Church alone, I had to sneak out of the house or else he would follow me. I was surprised to learn from his former owners that he once had dog obedience training. Maybe he was deaf for he never obeyed a word I said. As I worked in my yard, he was always just a few feet from me. He let me know when someone had driven into the driveway.

The first thing every morning I looked out the window onto the porch and there he was, waiting for me.

I have been told that the average life span for a

157

Song of Hope

big dog is around 11 or 12 years. Brutus entered his 15th year. Every morning as I looked out on the porch, I gave thanks to God for having him one more day.

Of course age changed his life. He could barely walk. I suspect he had a stroke for he had difficulty moving his back end. Our daily walk, instead of several miles, was merely to the mailbox and back moving at a snail's pace. On good days, when we ventured out of the yard, dogs challenged him. The deer ignored him. He was no longer king of the neighborhood.

I was placed in a dilemma. Finances were such that I could not afford to take him to a veterinarian. But what if he got really sick or indicated that he was in a great deal of pain? What if he had another stroke and couldn't move? How would I lift him into the car to even take him to the vet? I placed all my fears of the future into God's hands. I prayed that my dog would not suffer, that he would die a peaceful death here at home.

One day, when Brutus was moving slower than usual, I laid my hands upon his back and prayed that Jesus heal my dog, that he take away any pain that he might have. The presence of the Holy Spirit came over me and I could feel a force of energy between my hands and my dog. And Brutus got better.

I left on a trip, telling my son where to bury Brutus if he should die before I returned. I had picked out a spot in the corner of our wooded property. Each time I called home Matt reported that Brutus was OK and was even acting rather peppy.

Four months after I had prayed over my dog, the day before Thanksgiving, I looked out on the porch and Brutus wasn't there. We had three and 1/2 acres.

THE DEATH OF BRUTUS

Where would I find him? Had he wandered down the road or up on the mountainside to die? But somehow I knew. I walked directly to the spot where we had planned on burying him, and there, right there, lay Brutus.

My property used to be an ancient river bed. Rock is everywhere. Yet when I dug the hole, I didn't even need to use the crow bar or pick axe. I didn't hit one rock. Brutus was so heavy it took all my strength to drag him the few inches to the grave. If he had died any other place, I wouldn't have been able to move him. I wouldn't have been able to lift him into a wheel barrow.

Coincidence? Instinct? My dog just knew that he was going to die so he went over to this spot? I don't think so.

When fear of the future creeps over me, when I think for a moment that God doesn't care about the little things in my life, when I think my prayers aren't heard or answered, I remember my dog. God cares about the birds of the air and clothes the flowers of the field. He cares about us. He is with us always.

Eternal Father,
Thank you for caring for us,
for holding us in your hand.

CANCER!

In January my best friend, "Carey", was diagnosed with ovarian cancer. Was I going to lose another friend? Was I some sort of bad luck? Was God such a jealous God that any person that came into my life, and formed a friendship with me, was going to be taken from me in some way or another? I lost the love and friendship of my husband. I lost friends through the divorce because many couples are not comfortable with single women friends. I lost friends when I became religiously serious, because many are not comfortable around religiously enthusiastic persons. I lost friends who were religious but did not understand the spiritual journey I was on, and so labeled me satanic and dangerous.

I couldn't get rid of the thoughts that I was being punished in some way or that God was a jealous God and so was taking away a friend. Oh, how I prayed for the healing of my friend!

During the night I awoke in absolute stillness. One does not realize you can hear a constant ring in your ears until all is silent. One does not realize you can hear your blood flowing until all is silent. Into this silence I remembered the poem I was given, "In the stillness of the Lord, one hears His voice." I knew I was in the stillness of the Lord.

I said, "Speak, Lord, for your servant is listening," and into my mind came the words, "Lay your hands on Carey."

These were words I did not want to hear. I am very uncomfortable laying on hands. Maybe this stems from the accusations that I "shot" evil spirits into people. Maybe it comes from my lack of self-confidence — and lack of confidence in the Lord.

If I were to lay on hands, I had to be as pure as possible, an open channel of God's grace flowing through me. I could not have any barriers within me to stop this flow. One barrier was my fear that Carey's sickness was a punishment.

I went to my pastor. Hearing of my fears, he said, "That's a stupid thought, Kathy."

He prayed over me to remove these thoughts and gave me his blessing.

Dumb thoughts surface, doubts surface, even after numerous experiences of God's love and goodness.

I went to Carey and was very uncomfortable. She was faithful at Charismatic prayer meetings and told me what to do. Often when we pray together, Carey is given a prophetic word and this time was no different. She received, "Break open the Eucharist and share it." Then she said, "Kathy, do not be afraid to be part of the curing process."

In Charismatic circles the language has developed to explain different healings. To be "cured" means an instant healing, right then and there. "Healed" means a healing over time. But when I heard Carey say the word "curing" process, I thought of a farmer's wife who "cures" meat by adding salt, or "cures" pickles by adding many ingredients to cucumbers. It is a slow process involving many ingredients. To be part of the curing process can simply be giving witness, arousing curiosity, adding salt. Another person mentions a healing mass, more spices, and so they go. Persons have hands laid on them and are healed, but many were part of this curing process. Every person who gives witness, encourages the sick, encourages them to believe.

The next day I attended a program and the speaker talked about "breaking open a story and sharing it." This seemed to me to be the same as Carey's prophecy, the day before. I went to the speaker and asked her what that phrase meant.

She explained, "When you read a story you get one meaning. When you read it again you get a deeper meaning. The third time, and suddenly, "Aha!!" a new, deeper meaning emerges. This is breaking open a story."

Carey and I were receiving deeper and deeper meanings of Jesus in our lives. These meanings were not just for us. We were to share it — to break open the Eucharist and share it.

Carey was hit hard after her second chemo treatment. I came to see her and the first sight of someone very sick when you are used to their robust health is always a shock. She was in a great deal of pain and very nauseous. She could not get out of bed. She was self-conscious because she had lost her hair but her wig kept sliding off on her pillow. As I looked at her, suddenly everything physical about her disappeared and all I saw was beauty.

I cannot put into words what I saw. How can one

say they saw beauty without describing the object that
was beautiful? But I cannot say I saw any object or saw
anything different in the physical sense. With limited
words, all I can say is I saw beauty. Perhaps I saw her
soul, I don't know.

I think I saw her as Jesus sees her. As Jesus sees
us. He does not look merely at physical attributes we
have, nor at our talents or accomplishments. He looks at
us and sees beauty, as one who looks at something with
pure love.

Remember the expression, "She has a face only
her mother could love." Mothers overlook faults and
blemishes of their children. Straggly hair, banged up
knees, dirty faces are ignored. The child smiles and the
mother scoops them up and hugs them and kisses them,
dirt and all.

After this experience I found I had a great love
for Carey. I knew this love was beyond all human love I
had ever experienced and was not of human origin.

I tried to describe this love to Carey one day. This
love was almost more for my benefit, for I couldn't convey
it at all to her. A hug would not do. Words were inadequate. The only way I could show it was to visit her and
phone her as often as I could, to stand by her through
this sickness. Then I told her the words that came into
my mind as I drove to see her, words I believe Jesus
spoke:

"This love that you have for Carey, this love that I
have given you, is but a drop of water compared to the
ocean of love I have for her."

I told Carey I did not understand why she had
cancer, why she had to suffer so with her chemo treat-

ments. I believed, however, that God's love for her was so immense, beyond all words. Someday we would know why she had to suffer so.

Carey answered, "I have to live each moment then embraced in this love."

Jesus, we do not understand our sufferings.
Help us live each moment aware of your love.
Grant us Your love in our relationship with others.
Help us see and treat our children with this love.

HAWAII

My relatives planned a trip to Hawaii. I couldn't afford to go but couldn't afford not to go either. It was a family thing. Family means a lot to me. Six aunts and six cousins went. It was also a woman thing. No men allowed. My mom went and my sister. My other sister was going to go too, but at the last minute had to cancel out.

Two weeks before I went I had this dream: I was in the woods, walking along a path which followed a stream. As I walked, the stream overflowed its banks and covered the path. It became difficult walking, for I did not know where the smooth path was and was no longer sure of my footing. The water got deeper and pushed against the backs of my legs. I discovered that if I braced my feet like one does sliding down snow the river carried me and down the stream I went.

I was carried across a large body of water and across a bridge. On the other side of the bridge was a building on pilings. This building was like an emporium, it sold everything. There was a bar, a restaurant, clothing for sale, etc. A woman with black hair spoke to me, but when I awoke I did not remember what she said. I saw the Indian woman from the t.v. series, "Northern Exposure." I yelled, "Hey, Indian." She did not mind that I called her that. She cried, "Kathy!" and came and gave me a hug. End of dream.

165

Song of Hope

My sister and I flew from California and met the rest from Wisconsin on the island of Oahu. My sister and I attended one of these condo time-share sales talks in order to get tickets to the Polynesian Cultural Center for a great saving. They normally cost around $60 and we got them for $20 apiece for listening to this salesman's spiel for a couple of hours.

The salesman showed us a beautiful coffee table photo book featuring the island of Maui where the condos were located. As he turned the pages I suddenly said, "Stop! Turn back."

There before me was the building on pilings I had seen in my dream.

"Where is that picture taken?" I asked.

"The town of Lahaina."

I asked my sister, who was in charge of the travel plans, if we were going there. She answered, "We are going to the island of Maui, we will have a car, and we can go wherever we wish."

As soon as we arrived in Maui my mom, aunt, sister and I drove to Lahaina. I walked along the beach until I saw the building on pilings. Leading to it was the bridge in my dream. In reality it was a sea wall but it looked like a bridge.

I walked across that "bridge" and into my dream. The feeling of the Presence of the Holy Spirit came over me. It was a weird experience.

The building on pilings was a former fish cannery turned into numerous gift shops. There was a bar, a restaurant, clothing stores, etc. A woman in the end store spoke to me. She had black hair. She said, "You certainly are carrying a heavy burden." She meant my camera and camera bag.

I answered, "Sometimes it gets even heavier." I thought, but did not say out loud, "And sometimes God takes away all weight," as I remembered the hike to the mountains and He took away the weight of my camera and lunch bag. God will remove our burdens if we but let Him.

I went outside the shop and stood next to two Hawaiian women. I didn't have the nerve to say, "Hey Indian," to them. I didn't say anything at all.

I knew with this dream coming true I was supposed to be in Hawaii, whether I wanted to be or not, or could afford to be or not. I knew God was with me and guiding me.

My mom was 80 and the oldest of the aunts, but she was in the best shape. The rest had a very difficult time walking. My favorite cousin had been in a car wreck ten years before and was in constant pain. When you see your relatives for just a few hours every two to five years, you may know they are hurting but not realize how much. When you see the pain in their eyes, the perspiration running down their face after walking just half a block, love pours out to them. You feel very helpless. And so I prayed.

Religion was a taboo subject. I was told, "Jesus healed when he was alive but he's dead now. Other people do not heal." I answered, "They don't, but Jesus does through them."

My attempts to describe stories of healings were met with skepticism. They had a look in their eyes which said, "Here's someone who will buy the Brooklyn Bridge." Most had brought their rosaries and believed in prayer.

Song of Hope

I hoped to plant some seeds.

I wondered, "Do they have to ask for our prayers? Do they have to know that they are being prayed for? Do they have to have faith in the prayer? Do they have to be converted (grow in faith) because of any healing they experience?"

Doubts continued to pop into my mind. Yet I prayed.

My sister and I spent one week in Hawaii. The rest stayed for another week before flying back to Wisconsin. My sister heard the news first and called to tell me what happened.

On the flight home, my aunt had a heart attack. It was a non-stop flight to Chicago. They asked if there was a doctor on board, and just as in the movies, a doctor ministered to her. No one was allowed off the plane in Chicago until my aunt was taken into an ambulance. They would not allow my cousin to ride with them.

My cousin caught a taxi. The driver was a foreigner to Chicago and they got lost three times. He zoomed by the hospital, saw it, slammed on the brakes and was rear-ended.

My cousin was admitted to the hospital as a patient.

Whatever had been wrong with her neck and back was jolted back into place and she left the hospital pain-free.

My aunt had two angioplasties and returned home feeling much better.

God sometimes works in mysterious ways.

After several months, I called my aunt to see how they were doing. All was back to "normal". After all,

came the explanation, the muscles and everything over
ten years were atrophied and so the lack of pain was just
a fluke. And the doctor told my aunt that her arteries
would clog every three months and sure enough, that
was happening.

During my freshman year in college I played with
the paddle ball during free moments. A paddle ball is a
flat wooden paddle with a rubber band and a ball attached.
You could play with one of these things for a long time
before it broke. Sometimes when you hit the ball it went
every which way and then would fly back and hit the back
of the paddle. I learned that any accidental maneuver
could be learned and repeated. It is my belief that if
muscles could become pain free, they can stay pain free.

Father John Hampsh of California told of a healing
he witnessed. A group of people began praying over a
thalidomide baby, now a man. He had a hand growing
out of his shoulder. The group prayed for twenty minutes,
when suddenly the arm began to grow. They continued
to pray until the arm was grown out to full length. If
new bone and muscles and blood vessels could grow,
then atrophied muscles could be healed.

Nuns from St. Joseph Prayer Ministry in Washington
told of a time when they prayed over a deaf man. He
regained his hearing completely, but when he went to
leave, he grabbed his hearing aids and said, "Just in case."
He was deaf by the time he reached the door.

We went to Hawaii in October. The following
February my mother died. My time with her in Hawaii
was the last time I had with her. As I said, her health
was in the best shape. I never dreamed she would be
the first to go. My younger sister who could not come

to Hawaii flew to Texas and spent Christmas with my parents, so she, too, had a chance for a good, last visit with Mom.

Eternal Father, grant me faith in Your healings through Your Son that I may be healed.

FIRE!

On Friday Nov. 17 my Benedictine friend had back surgery. Another friend, Marilyn, was having hospital tests. I spent the day in prayer. In the afternoon about 2:00 I raked leaves for a while and then my neighbor said to me, from over the fence, that he was planting 3000 redwood trees. This was the first time he had ever spoken to me.

I raked and I thought. I keep envisioning fruit trees and roses every time I look at one of my fields. This is ridiculous because fruit trees don't do that well in this valley, the deer find roses a favorite delicacy and I want that field clear for a horse again someday. Yet, when I look at the field, I see fruit trees and roses. I am not an imaginative person, so this seems weird to me. I cannot even explain what I mean when I say I see this, for I don't really. I can't explain it.

I was thinking of all this and prayed, "Lord, do you want me to plant these things?"

I got no answer, but after a while asked my neighbor if he had ever planted trees. He said no. He just had this impulse to plant 3000 redwood trees. His wife said she thought the idea utterly ridiculous.

I said, "I was thinking I should plant my field with fruit trees. Do you think I should burn it first?" He didn't answer whether or not I should burn it, but remarked that if I did I shouldn't worry about it spreading to his side of my property, for there was nothing to burn. On my side, with lawn, it wouldn't spread. But the neighbor's field to the west was tinder-dry tall grass. The wind usually came from the west so I had better start at that end of my field. He suggested now was a good time to do it, because it was going to rain in three days. He said days, but maybe he meant hours. The thought of rain did not occur to me. It was a beautiful day.

It was November 17 and we still had not had any fall rains. The grass in the field was tinder dry.

I decided to burn it right then. It was 3:30 p.m. I got a broom, shovel and hose ready and set the grass on fire at the northwest side. A grass fire only burns at the perimeter. This fire started off slowly toward the east. Then I heard, high overhead, the sound that I thought was a huge jet. Suddenly the wind swooped down and with one mighty gust whipped the fire to the west - into my neighbor's field. There it roared, four feet high, straight toward my neighbor's open faced hay barn!

I scrambled over the fence where the bear had knocked it down, so I didn't have to climb up and over it, tripped and fell, and as I rolled up, I prayed, "Lord, help me."

The prayer no sooner left my lips when the wind immediately died and with a few slaps of my broom the fire was out.

I continued to burn a small triangle of my field, the wind barely blowing it to the east. That took about half an hour before it went out.

I then lit another section of the field, again starting on the west side. This time I quickly beat it out along side the fence so it wouldn't back burn. The fire burned slowly, very slowly, toward the east. I thought this was going to take days to burn. I thought I was awful stupid to be burning this field alone. I should have waited until a day my son was home. I also thought it was beginning to spread out too far, I ought to start beating out the edges, when again, I heard this sound of a jet coming from high in the sky. I knew now that it was no jet.

Now that I had experienced no control over a grass fire once the wind hit it, I was scared stiff and prayed, "God, help me with this fire."

With a swoop the wind grabbed that fire and drove it eastward. It roared four feet high. There was absolutely no way I could have stopped it. It burned east and a little north until it came near the edge of the field, then the wind turned and blew south and drove the fire in a straight line. When the fire was four feet from the south fence, it turned and blew the fire west until it was about six feet from the west fence.

The moment that fire turned for the third time and headed west I knew I was witnessing an awesome sight. I knew I was witnessing the power of God within that heat and wind.

I danced with that fire. As I moved toward it, it moved away. As I backed up, it flared brightly where it was.

I stopped and stood. I was nothing compared to it. I was before God displaying His power and His might before me.

Suddenly dying down, the fire burned slowly, a tiny line four feet from the south fence and six feet from the west fence.

Song of Hope

I drew an imaginary line two feet from the south fence and thought, "When the fire reaches there I'll put it out with the broom" and prayed, "Lord, please don't let the wind catch it and blow it past that two feet."

When the fire hit this imaginary line, which still had leaves and grass in it, it went out, poof.

I only had the far southwest corner to burn. There were about twelve little fires going in that corner, plus there was a big fire in the middle of the field where a pile of sticks was burning. I was just thinking of putting out these little fires, when, poof, they all went out at once, even the large center fire. They went out as if a candle snuffer had dropped down upon them.

I stood there, and said, "Lord, what about all these little sparks lying here and there amongst the leaves? A wind could fan them into flames during the night."

I no sooner thought this when it started to rain, just like that. It continued to rain all night and continued for several days. Everything turned sopping wet. My field would have been impossible to burn.

To witness such a miracle of wind and fire was absolutely awesome! To realize my lack of control, my littleness and God's greatness manifested before me is indeed awesome, mind boggling.

I was in the house before 5:30 with my field burned in a nice square way.

Eternal Father, we sing a song of hope.
Hope that indeed, You are with us
and are holding us in Your hands.

THE ICE CREAM TRUCK

I went to church for a Holy Hour. As I got out of the car, I heard the music of an ice cream truck! An ice cream truck was in our little town? I looked and sure enough. Down the street came an ancient ice cream truck. The words, "Sharon's Ice Cream For Children" were written on the side. I thought, "Oh nuts. It's for children. I sure would like an ice cream bar." But I'm a stickler for rules, and the sign on the truck said, "For Children."

As I sat in the church, into my mind came the words, "Go and lay hands on Marilyn." Was this thought from God or from my own imagination? I figured it wouldn't hurt if I carried it out. I asked the Lord, "Now?" and into my mind came, "Now."

In my story of the fire, I mentioned that Marilyn was in the hospital for tests. She was diagnosed with primary pulmonary hypertension. She lived with her medicine attached to her at all times, a computer regulating the dosage.

I went home to give Marilyn a call. Before I picked up the phone, I asked, "Do I go now? Can't I wait until after supper?" Into my mind came, "Now." I tracked Marilyn to her mother's. She knew that I had gone to the church for a Holy Hour. She often encouraged me to do so, saying that was the prayer form given to me by God. She excitedly asked me if anything happened, for

Song of Hope

often God revealed Himself to me in some way during this quiet time with Him. I told her, "I'm to come and pray with you."

"Oh, good," she said. "I'll be home by the time you get there."

Marilyn lived fifteen miles from me. As I drove I thought of my fear of laying hands on people. Into my mind came the thoughts, "If you knew that if you laid hands on someone, they would be healed, would you do it?" I answered, "Yes, of course."

The thoughts continued in my mind. "What if there were five people, and you knew that if you laid hands on all five, that only one would be healed, would you still lay hands on all five, for the sake of that one?" I answered, "Yes, I would."

"What if there were ten people, and you knew that if you laid hands on all ten, that only one would be healed, would you still lay hands on all ten, for the sake of that one?" I answered, "Yes, of course."

The thought came, "Bingo."

Marilyn and I prayed together and when I said I had to leave, Marilyn asked, "Do you want a popsicle?" I said, "I'd love one." And Marilyn pulled out of the refrigerator an ice cream bar! She said that as she was coming home from her mom's, she got the strong urge to run into the store and get an ice cream bar for me.

God confirmed that He does communicate with us in our thoughts and does reward us with our actions.

Dear Lord, help me be silent to listen.
Help me be responsive to your call.

FANNING THE FLAME
PENTECOST RETREAT

This retreat, held at our parish, was a very powerful experience for many. Friday Night with Jesus Ministries, who helped the parish organize the retreat, received many phone calls from people who gave witness to the continuing effect of the Holy Spirit in their lives, long after it was over. This retreat was very powerful in my own life, and in a way, another turning point in my life.

First of all, I knew this retreat was going to be a powerful experience for me. Every person who had entered my life within the previous four years in a major way religiously was there. I was first Baptized in the Spirit under Father Campoli, who was one of the speakers. My spiritual director was there, my pastor was there.

My best friends, Carey and Marilyn, were there as were friends from several prayer groups, powerful friends, prayer partners.

Charlie Knecht, director of Friday Night with Jesus Ministry, and his wife Iris were there and other friends that I have met when attending Charismatic conferences throughout the Sacramento diocese.

I usually took very good notes since I wrote about these events for the Catholic Herald and for Friday Night with Jesus Ministries' newsletter, but this time I didn't. I spent hours playing the tapes made at the retreat, transcribing the messages given, and I knew I was supposed to do this, for every word went straight to my heart, again and again and again.

Iris opened the retreat with the vision statement and her words that particularly hit me were: "...to bring the healing power of Jesus here so that you may experience this power...to become people God has called us to be..."

I felt God was calling me and I was ready to say yes, but for what? To do what? I felt so powerless. Sister Maura's words gave me ease, "Many people in scripture responded to God by saying, "Here I am". They were often afraid, confused, not sure what they should do ... Real faith and real trust is called for."

Could I trust? Father John Campoli said our prayers must always end with a letting go, "Not my will, but yours be done".

He said: "Can we let go of our desire to understand everything and just trust?"

Who was this God I was asked to trust? Sister Janel answered that.

"Jesus is called the revelation of God. Jesus revealed God to us...A God who was loving...a God who was faithful...a God who understands...A God who loved us to death...A God who said the kingdom of God is among you."

Sister Margaret talked of the power of prayer. It has been documented that prayer has a place in healing. Linda Perkins gave witness, "I was healed of cancer through the prayers of my parish and of my friends."

Sister Janel read the gospel of Mark 10:46 about the healing of the blind beggar Bartimaeus. As she read, we were asked to think about our own blindness that needed to be healed. I saw my fear, my lack of trust, as my blindness. But my biggest fear was that if I give my life to God, it won't be good enough, and He will turn me down.

Sister Gloria, as a mime, acted out the gospel reading. When I saw that the mime was blind, I no longer looked at her. I have always had a hard time looking people in the eyes. Words, which I believe were whispered to me by Jesus, entered my mind, "If you don't look at people, how can you see others as I see them?"

Father Campoli said, "When God looks into your face, God sees His own reflection. And He says, 'You are so special, so precious to me. So precious to me that I gave my only son, Jesus, so that you could have life. You are so precious to me, that I poured forth the Spirit of my son, Jesus, to fill the life of each one of you...and I want you to rejoice tonight in the call of the Lord, calling each one of us to say yes."

Father John mentioned the many burdens that we can take upon ourselves, but the burden Jesus places on our shoulders is the burden of mercy, of forgiveness. We must forgive over and over and over again.

I know that giving one's life over to God is not easy for every time I turn around I have some close friend or family member tell me how stupid I am. These remarks, showing a lack of understanding, really hurt, and I must forgive over and over and over again.

Father John mentioned the many effects of the Spirit. One was that we become His instruments. A union is formed with others in the bond of love, and we hunger for the word of God. We become bold in our witness and we receive the Charism of Service.

179

Song of Hope

The more I listened the more I took on the attitude, "God really is calling me into His service. He won't turn me down and in my weakness, my imperfection, His strength will shine forth. Go for it, Kathy."

Sunday night after the retreat, when all the activity was over with and all my company gone, it was so silent, so lonely in my house and all my fears of the future came tumbling out as I cried. The same thing Monday night. "Please, Lord, take away these fears." And Tuesday morning I awoke filled with such peace, such joy, such love - and no more fear.

Eternal Father, I give you my willingness to leave this beautiful valley in reparation for those who do not see your hand in the beauty around them. I give you my willingness to leave my home in reparation for those who do not offer you a place in their homes. I give you all my possessions in reparation for those whose possessions keep them from following you. I give you my life for those who do not have the time to do so. I give you my fear of the future to give glory to You who leads all men.

June 18, 1996.

I GIVE MY LIFE TO GOD

I wrote a letter to my bishop, giving him my life, as God's representative on Earth. I wrote, saying, "Where does the church need me? Tell me what to do and I will do it. Tell me where to go and I'll go there."

I also listed my house for sale. My intentions were not necessarily to give all to God, but rather, because for four years, all doors remained shut to me. I could not get a job, and I placed my house for sale in order to pay my bills.

I had two friends, nuns in the prayer ministry, and they said to me, "Every time the words 'house of prayer' comes up, your name comes up."

The next day the book I was reading mentioned 'house of prayer'. On day three I asked my friends, "What is a house of prayer? I have never heard of one." They suggested I ask the nuns.

Day four the two nuns, Sister Mary Frances and Sister Mary Matthew, described several versions of a house of prayer.

Day seven I told this story to a friend of mine in Mt. Shasta and she said that just that morning she learned there was a house of prayer in Klamath Falls.

On day ten I learned there was a house of prayer in Vacaville. I was told, "Kathy, this is how God is calling

181

you, by having many people present you with the same idea. Listen."

I prayed, "Lord, if you want me associated, in any way, shape, or form, with a house of prayer, have the bishop write the words, 'house of prayer' in his letter to me."

The bishop wrote me a full page letter. He said we are all called to ministry, by our baptism and our confirmation. Some people are given a call to even greater work. But that is not his job to determine. One has to discern for themselves.

Paragraph four reads, "For some reason, it occurs to me, to suggest, that you might want to visit, ... the house of prayer in Vacaville."

I drove immediately to Vacaville and met with the Sister in charge of the house of prayer there. After prayer and discussion, she felt that I was not called to join her house of prayer, but rather, God had His own plans for me. Perhaps it was to have a house of prayer in my own home. I had placed it in God's hands when I placed it on the market. She encouraged me to continue my life of prayer. God would guide me.

Nothing happened. My life remained on hold. No job. Very few people came to look at my house. No buyers. And no one came to the house for prayer. Before this, many people came. Now only one at a time came, even though I had it in the bulletin every week for four months. I couldn't find a publisher for this book, and so I kept adding stories to it. Another year passed.

I felt if a theologian, a scripture scholar would read the book, publishers would then consider it. My two friends in the prayer ministry recommended that I ask

Father Nigro to read the manuscript. I had never heard of Father Nigro. He agreed to read my manuscript.

A friend came to visit and we prayed for God's direction and guidance in our lives. We prayed giving God thanksgiving for everything. Thank you, God, that we have no job. Thank you that our money is now all gone. Thank you that our books aren't accepted by any publisher. We thank you for everything in our lives, the bad as well as the good and we give glory to you, for you are with us and are guiding us."

We paused for breath, and the phone rang. It was Father Nigro. He said, "Kathy, I liked your manuscript very much and I wrote the preface to your book." It took a long time for that to sink in. I asked him what he thought God was calling me to do. He replied, "I think you should get a Masters in Theology to go along with your spiritual experiences."

That was Friday night.

Father gave me several universities and home studies to look into. Over the next several days I compared prices and course offerings and time to complete a Masters degree.

One friend, Cliff, without knowing what was happening in my life, said to me, "On the way to see you, I was given this thought to say to you; "The hardest thing to know is when to take action and when not to."

I asked another friend, "Sister, do you think I should get a Masters Degree?"

She answered, "Try the door. If it opens, go through it."

Well, the door opened, and I didn't step through it, I was sucked through it!

183

Song of Hope

I told my friend, who was staying with me and praying, "I can't go anywhere without a hair permanent."

She said, "Spokane is the beauty parlor capital of the world!"

I answered, "I don't care. I like my own beautician."

She said, "God is calling you and you want a permanent?"

I said, "Yes."

Late Wednesday afternoon we walked into the beauty parlor. My beautician doesn't work on Thursdays and Fridays are always booked solid with her regular customers. She showed me her calendar. Friday afternoon was blocked off. "I wanted to go camping this weekend but my husband just called and said we can't go until Saturday morning. I can do your hair on Friday." She went home and said to her husband, "Do you know that you are an answer to prayer?"

That Friday morning the Dean of Graduate Studies at Gonzaga University assured me he would do everything he could to help get me into the Masters of Spirituality program. By Friday evening I had a place to stay and a job in Spokane.

Saturday I worked at the Arts Guild.

I had been wishing to see my former pastor again. He had been transferred in June, right after the Pentecost retreat and at the time that I wrote the letter to the Bishop giving him my life. I knew that Father was on vacation, so I couldn't even call him and tell him the latest development in my life.

Sunday morning he walked into our church and sat down in the last pew! My church friends planned a potluck for Sunday afternoon, which turned into a farewell party for me, and both priests were able to attend.

I left early the next morning for Spokane, September 1, 1997.

My friends in my parish came and packed everything in my house and placed it all in storage and I placed my house for rent.

First of all, my job fell through in Spokane. Father Nigro tried to get me others, but they didn't work out. Father has a sister who is a nun in the same order as my two friends in the prayer ministry. I met her, and said, "I know two sisters of your order."

She said, "Did you know Sister Frances just had a stroke? You didn't? Would you like to use the phone?"

I called and Sister Matthew said, "Now will you come and live with us?"

I said, "Wait a minute! I just got to Gonzaga two weeks ago!"

Lord, help me know when to act and when not to!

TWO NUNS IN MY LIFE

Two nuns entered my life in 1995. In January I had a
terrible pain in my side. I prayed about it and opened
the Bible to a random page. I opened to Ezekiel, where
it describes a pain in his side. I don't know how many
places in the Bible it mentions pain in the side, but I
opened right to this description. Ezekiel was given a
pain in his side, one day for every year of Israel's sinfulness. Since this was January, the anniversary month of
Wade vs. Row, I thought perhaps my pain was for every
year of the sinful state our country has been in.

At the end of the month, on a Friday, friends from
the Trinity Prayer Community offered me a series of tapes
to watch on the healing ministry. Carol said, "Since you
aren't doing anything anyway." Jeannie added, "And
don't watch them alone."

The next day my son had a ski tournament and
he wanted me to come and watch. As the day went on,
my pain got worse. By supper time, I could barely move,
the pain was intense and I had no energy. Gail and I
chatted and she told me of a miracle that happened in
her family. I recorded this miracle earlier in this book,
about her brother-in-law driving off a cliff and hanging
upside down for hours. A light around the car guided a
person to it, he was found, and miraculously recovered.

I said to Gail, "I have been given about twenty

video tapes on the healing ministry. Would you like to come and watch them with me?"

She said yes and we agreed upon Thursday evenings at 7:00.

It wasn't until the next day that I realized that from that moment on, the pain in my side was gone. When I walked to the car after the tournament, I had no pain, and I was filled with energy.

I invited several people whom I suspected had the gift of healing. I told them that they should watch these tapes to see what the Catholic church says about this ministry, which entails far more than just laying on of hands. Word spread and nine people came to my house Thursday evening. Some of them I did not even know, others I barely knew. My friend from the ski resort was never able to come.

Two nuns had recorded these tapes. As we watched one said that the viewing of the video tape should be followed by an hour long session of prayer. I thought, "Lord, I don't know these people. How do you ask people you don't know to just pray. I don't know if they have little children, babysitters expecting them home at a certain time. Lord, this is yours. You have to handle it."

Later in the tape, one of the nuns told of an incident that during an hour of silent prayer someone was healed. I prayed, "Lord, how do you ask people to pray in silence? How do you explain contemplative prayer? Lord, this is yours. I don't know what to say. You have to handle it."

When the tape ended, I got up, turned off the t.v. and the v.c.r. and said, "We will pray now." I sat down and immediately was enveloped by the Holy Spirit. I

187

could think and I could hear, but I could not move or speak. I thought, "Lord, thank you for this hug, but I have to lead the prayer now."

When I remained in this state, I prayed, "Lord, if you don't want me to lead the prayer, please place in someone else's mind to start it. This is my home and people are waiting for me."

We sat in silence for twenty minutes! No one moved. No one even shuffled their feet.

The tapes covered the prayer ministry and taught how to pray with people. "What do you want Jesus to do for you?" The intention of the teachers was to have the newly formed prayer group make themselves available within their parish. Most groups set up a place after their church service. One person "fished" for two legged fish, encouraging people to come for prayer. Two people did the actual vocal praying with the people and a fourth silently interceded.

At the end of the course, the two nuns came to our area to personally meet us. That is how I met Sister Mary Matthew and Sister Mary Frances. They stayed at my house and we hit it off immediately. It seemed as if we had always known each other. We talked often of my coming to stay with them, not on a permanent basis but rather a chance for me to learn from them. Once when they prayed for me, Sister Frances said she had a vision of a globe with a pen going around it.

It was in 1995 that I met the two nuns, that I had the dream come true in Hawaii, and God burned my field.

In 1996 I wrote the letter to the Bishop and put my house up for sale. I knew that God was guiding me, and that maybe I had to get rid of my house in order to follow Him. I had no idea where I would go or what I would do if my house sold. The two sisters offered me a place to stay until God showed me direction. This gave me hope that I would at least have a roof over my head.

In September, 1997, Sister Frances had a major stroke. I called to see how she was and Sister Matthew said, "Now will you come and live with us?"

The following weekend I drove across the state of Washington to talk about this with Sister Matthew.

Lord, I believe, I adore, I hope, and I trust in You.
Please remove my unbelief, my lack of love,
my doubt, my lack of trust.
I beg pardon for those who do not believe,
do not adore, do not hope nor trust in You.

CALLED

I gave my life to God. I said, "Where does the Church
need me. Tell me where to go and I will go there. Tell
me what to do and I will do it." Our God is an awesome
God! He cannot be outdone in giving. He guides us. He
is with us always.

God connected me with Sister Mary Matthew and
her prayer ministry. When we prayed together, asking if
this was part of God's plan, that we be together, we both
became filled with the Holy Spirit at the same time, and
it left us at the same time.

When I was leaving to return to college at Spokane,
my whole life flashed before my eyes and I saw that
everything that had happened enabled me to say yes to
this ministry. Even my inability to get a job made me free.

When God began revealing Himself to me, I
thought that this happened only to holy people, to
priests and religious. I said to God, "Does this mean
You want me to become a nun? I don't want to be one,
but I will, if that is what You want. I will investigate
and learn what I can, but You have to do Your part, and
give me the desire."

I took the Lay Ministry program, a three year program offered by the Diocese of Sacramento because it
helped one discern a call to the religious life. I talked to
the director of vocations and learned that most orders

require that a person's youngest child be 21 before they are accepted. This gave me several years to pray about this vocation. I visited several convents and I expected that if this is what God wanted me to do, He would let me know. The ground would shake or I would get an overwhelming desire to be there.

While doing my laundry at Gonzaga, I prayed and asked God if He wanted me to join Sister Matthew. If so, please give me the desire. Such an overwhelming desire to join her came over me, that I wanted to get up and leave right then and there! This was the feeling that I expected when I visited various convents, but never got. I knew that God wanted me in this ministry, but when? Three months from now, after I have a foothold in the Master's program; a year from now, after I have my degree?

Everyone encouraged me to stay in college. Only one person thought I should leave immediately. Father Campoli saw God's plan in all of this. I asked, "But if God wanted me to be with Sister, why would He have Sister Frances die now? Why not three months from now, or a year from now?"

Father asked, "Gonzaga is all part of His plan. Would you have left your beautiful valley, your friends otherwise, if you were set and stable there? You could leave them for a year, and now that you have left, it is easier to make the permanent move. Gonzaga provided the impetus for you to leave."

I still pondered and prayed. I confided my dilemma to one of the women living in the college house with me and she said, "Just ask Jesus what to do. You are doing it for Him. He will tell you. Just ask Him."

Song of Hope

I prayed in bed, "Jesus, what do You want me to do? Place something in one of my hands." I lifted up my right hand. "Should I stay?" I lifted up my left hand. "Or should I go?"

Right hand - stay. Left hand - go. I felt something in my left hand.

I said, "This is probably my own imagination. Lord, You know what I need to know that it is from You. Should I stay, or should I go?" Immediately into my mind came the words, "Go to the world with my Word," followed by a tremendous rush of the Holy Spirit over me and I rested in the Spirit right there in my room.

I joined Sister Matthew on October 16, 1997.

When I was first Baptized in the Holy Spirit , I had seven visions of seven objects over a period of several days. The visions were projected on the back of my eyelids. The object was placed in silhouette in front of a round bright light. The object was moved to get my attention, for normally I do not look at the back of my eyelids. Once identified, the vision was gone. All the objects became important symbols in my life, and I thought that was why God permitted me to have such visions.

The seven objects were a rosary, Mary, the Host above the Chalice, the Monstrance, the Sacred Heart of Jesus, the Crown of Thorns, and the Infant Jesus of Prague.

After I joined Sister, as I sat in the chapel at her house of prayer, I became aware that there, before me, were all seven objects! On the tabernacle door was the Host above the Chalice with rays of light shooting from it. I went and got my paper with the drawings of the objects, and it was identical.

God blessed me again by letting me know that He was guiding me.

When we went to Alaska, my first speaking trip, Sister assigned to me the topics, "The Love of the Father," and "Prayer."

When I packed for Gonzaga, I had very little time, and I had to get everything in my small Ford Escort, including my computer and printer. It was amazing that the things I chose were just exactly what I needed. I had brought with me those drawings. I also brought with me my notes from the silent retreat I had made in 1994. While looking over them, I noticed a prayer that I wrote and had forgotten completely.

"Lord, this is what I want.

"I do not know if this is what You want.

"1. I want to live where I am living now.

"2. I want to be able to write about and speak about Your love and about prayer.

"3. I want to be Your instrument through which people receive the Holy Spirit and Your love.

"Lord, I do not know if this is also what You want. If it is, You will have to bring it about, for I have no idea how to do it."

Our awesome God answered that prayer!

Sister and I prayed with someone, and as she prayed aloud I thought of what I would say come my turn, and Sister said it. I thought of something else, and Sister said it. This happened for five things! It is awesome when God molds you into a team through the Holy Spirit.

Song of Hope

Every day someone came for prayer. I began to witness miracles occurring right before my eyes. People would enter the house literally shaking, and leave filled with peace.

A young teenager came with a friend for prayer. The young girl hardly said a word, but she quietly said to me that her parents were getting a divorce. She was hurting so much from this, that she could not speak. Afterwards we heard from her family that she returned home so filled with peace that everyone asked, "What gives? Your life is upside down, yet you are so filled with peace." She answered, "Why don't you try Jesus on for size?"

Later we heard that her parents got back together again, and she became passionately in love with God.

Another time a young mother came with her children. Her husband wanted another woman. He didn't want counseling. He didn't want to talk about it. His mind was made up. She returned the next day and the next. We are not into marriage counseling. All we did was pray with her, encouraging her to forgive, which she and her children readily did.

On the fourth day she called and said that her husband wanted to talk. She didn't want to be alone with him and a restaurant was too public. Could she come to the house?

Sister ushered them into the chapel and as they prayed, the man broke down and cried. He said he was sorry for sinning against God and his family and he asked for forgiveness. He wanted his family back.

This was God's doing. This was God touching a heart and soul. Frankly, I personally did not have much hope for this marriage. God showed me once again that with Him all things are possible.

People who had come for prayer years ago and were healed of drug addictions and alcoholism, returned with their friends.

One teenage boy told us he was quite tired of living for his parents. When he was young he was curious and excited about everything, but through the influence of his parents, trying to please them, he became quiet and subdued. He wanted to burst out of these bonds and discover who he really was. I told him to participate in the extreme games in Australia, or become a missionary and help other people. That would let him know who he was, but he didn't have to turn toward sin to discover who he was.

In the first ten months Sister and I traveled to Alaska, California three times, Oregon six times, Montreal, Nova Scotia and Newfoundland and drove to Wisconsin, giving Life in the Spirit Seminars, talks on prayer, and praying with people.

In 1994 I had a vision of two medals. One was the Miraculous Medal, the other was of the Infant Jesus of Prague. I thought God wanted me to have these. The Miraculous Medal was easy to obtain. I thought I got the Infant Jesus medal at the convent in Minnesota, but when I looked more closely at it, it was, "Our Lady of Olives, Protect us from storms and floods."

A friend was going to Prague, Czechoslovakia and I asked her to obtain a medal for me. She became too sick to go into that country but a friend gave her a medal, but alas, she lost it.

Another friend went there two times to see relatives

but she was not a Catholic and returned both times with other religious articles, but not the medal of the Infant of Prague.

When I was in Montreal, Sister Rosa Bedard, a Presentation sister, gave me both medals. God let me know once again that I was supposed to be there. He was guiding me. Our God is an awesome God.

When I prayed alone, it was powerful, but whenever I joined a group or when I had a prayer partner, it was awesome! Scripture says, "Where two or more are gathered in my name, there am I in your midst." It also says, "Go to your closet and pray." It is not either or, but both. My friend, Marilyn, and I would pray together on the phone. She usually did the speaking, but gradually I began to say aloud what was in my heart. But I began to feel comfortable praying with people, trusting that God will give me the words, just a few weeks before I joined Sister Mary Matthew.

I am a pray-er gatherer. When my son, Bob, had an accident, I called all my friends, and asked them for prayer. I knew their prayer groups were praying for their intentions, and in a few minutes I had several hundred people praying for Bob. When I pray with Sister Mary Matthew, I figure there are several thousand people praying for our intentions. Everyone who has taken the prayer ministry classes, attended our retreats, or told us that they are praying for us, unite with us in prayer. We need one another. We need each other's prayers, all the way to heaven. We need the strength, the nourishment of gathering in prayer communities, as well as the silence of praying, and listening, alone.

Every year since the seventies, I attended Bible

study classes, first with the Bereans, and then with the Catholics when they started having one. The priest also attended and instructed us. We began studying the new Catechism as soon as it was printed in English. We were blessed with very knowledgeable priests who explained carefully each section. We were lucky to cover a page in the two hours that we met. I also listened to teachings on scripture audio tapes, recorded by Father James Nisbet. I took the three year Lay Ministry program and learned about church history, scripture, and spiritual direction. Every month for one year I was able to attend a Charismatic retreat, learning even more about the Roman Catholic religion, the Trinity within us, the gifts of the Holy Spirit. Father Michael Brennan said, "Give God permission to change your life." Father John Hampsh taught the importance of forgiveness and healing of memories and the family tree. Father John Campoli stressed the love God has for each of us within the present moment. Father Stephen Barham emphasized the healing in the Eucharist. That is Jesus, the Son of God, right there. And He will heal us. Father Jerry Bevilacqua taught that the great temptation in times of trial, is to blame God, to not give Him thanks for all things. Father Rick Thomas had us give all of our problems to the Lord, to dump them in the basket and leave them there. Father Lou Cerelli emphasized the beauty of healing during the Mass. Bishop Sam Jacobs had an altar call, to come forward and publically give our lives to Jesus. I read numerous books on spirituality.

All this training and study, plus my experiences, prepared me for the speaking and prayer ministry in which God placed me. Nothing is by accident.

Song of Hope

My longing for a prayer partner, for someone to go with me to Mass, as well as someone to share a meal, watch the sunrise, a thunder storm, and the ocean waves, was fulfilled. I left a beautiful valley, but God placed me near the Puget Sound. I left many wonderful friends, but God gave me many, many more, all spirit filled. An old Girl Scout song reminds me, "Make new friends, but keep the old. One is silver and the other gold."

I am a very shy person. I had to get rid of this constant thinking of myself, of what other people thought of me, in order to step out in faith and trust. Toastmasters, an organization to train public speakers, gave me the courage, as did the Acting, Directing, Playwriting class. But many times Sister and I would be asked to speak, and we had to depend upon the Lord to give us the words. Once, we had a speech planned but when we were introduced, they announced it as something else. We had three minutes to change our minds, and we weren't able to communicate it to each other.

One time I was speaking to a group of 30 men at Monroe prison when my mind went blank. Sister Mary Matthew prompted me with what I just said. Nothing. She prompted with where I was going. Nothing. I silently prayed, "Lord, I am standing here for You. Give me the words You want me to say."

I began speaking and when I finished the men enthusiastically applauded. Sister, and the chaplain, came over and told me that what I said, after I changed the direction of my speech, touched several men. I could not remember what I had said at all.

Sister Mary Matthew and I traveled to the island

of Trinidad and gave a retreat to 160 women on "Healing the Father Relationship." We stressed the need for forgiveness. Afterwards several gave witness of a healing they experienced. One elderly woman said that for the first time she could forgive the man who raped her when she was a young child, and for the first time the pain in her stomach left. Another lady said she could now hear. Praise be to God.

It is an honor and a privilege to be called by God. He calls each one of us. Do not be afraid. Simply say, "Here I am. Send me."

Lord, I give You my hope. I give You my dreams.
I give You my life as a tool. I give You my life.
I give You my love. These are my gifts to You.

Song of Hope

Kathy Flanagan Moore

People will react in different ways to what I have recorded in these pages. Some, even though they have not experienced anything like this, will just know they are loved by God all the more.

It is this love that we cling to in times of trials. It is this message of hope that we cling to as we try to trust that God is holding us in His hands, that He is guiding us, that He does love us beyond any love we can fathom.

Living in the rural mountains of Northern California, I met at least two people a week who gave testimony of how God touched their lives. If I could meet these many people, just think of the thousands God is Manifesting His Presence to, every day. Our God is an awesome God.